IDEOLOGY IN TURKISH CINEMA

IDEOLOGY IN TURKISH CINEMA

Mustafa Mencütekin

BLUE DOME

New Jersey

17 16 15 14   1 2 3 4

Published by Blue Dome Press
335 Clifton Avenue
Clifton, NJ 07011

www.bluedomepress.com

Library of Congress Cataloging-in-Publication Data Available

ISBN: 978-1-935295-50-1

Printed by
Imak Ofset, Istanbul - Turkey

Contents

"Real life is becoming indistinguishable from the movies."

(Adorno and Horkheimer, 1972:126)

Introduction: To Somewhere Where the Last Word Does Not Exist

Prendergast defines the film as "a work of art, the product of creative intention. Inasmuch as the artist's vision is informed by myth, ideology, or personal biography, interpretation opens out into multiple dimensions" (1986:243), Dworkin sees the cinema 'as the most glamorous exemplar of mass-oriented, technologically-produced media' (1977:96), while Ruppert points out the multi-dimensional aspect of the cinema in the way that "the "cinematic apparatus" is shaped by technological, cultural, and historical determinants; viewers are identified by class, gender, and various interpretive and ideological priorities" (1989:29), still Williams focuses on the part of audience endeavoring to describe the nature of film as "[it] is not what happens on the screen, but what happens between the audience and the screen" (1971:8). Whatever points are focused or neglected regarding the definition or description of the cinematic art, the main issue of the cinema seems to be too much dependent on "how the cinema works to construct, interpellate and reproduce its viewer as subject, how it solicits actual moviegoers to identify with and through ideologically marked positions of subjectivity (Hansen, 1993:197). The varying processes of mediation which is closely affiliated with the cinematic creation are 'inextricably intertwined' with ideology; and since "mediation is an ideological process, whilst ideology becomes visible the moment that mediation processes are pinned down" (Buckingham, 1986:81), "the semiotics of film itself [becomes] ideological in several senses" (Henderson, 1975:20).

In today's from-all-aspects chaotic life, when some claim great narratives have reached to an end with "the end of history," one claim is surely out of suspect: ideology is based and dominant in both circles of complicated individuality and sociality. In today's somehow post-modernized social life, it a division is expected to have been already constructed through a proper classification between art and industry, culture and entertainment, meaning and profit. However, the division and its discriminations achieved so far are not able to function so as to challenge the economic, ideological and aesthetic bases of the cinematic institution as it unfortunately exists in today's life. As of the nature of cinema—as both a sort of art, communication and technology—Caroll argues that "motion pictures [are] our dominant mass art, one that is so widespread, internationally pervasive, and accessible across boundaries of class and culture" (1985:80), that naturally directs us to search for the link between ideology in general and the cinematic art. There has been of course no coincidence that "many writers from the 1920s ... invented a range of metaphors to describe film as a language or a universally intelligible form," and in this way, "historians of film theory have characterized this response as 'the celebration of film as a new "universal language" '(Frey, 2010:324). Where 'a universal language' is in concern, there stands a must to seek for the ideological conception. Whereas "a film text is only a means for communicating a set of values and ideas and whether these ideas are political or not, the film still embodies ideological precepts," the link between a film and ideology may or may not be direct or open, "in most cases, a given film will translate the dominant ideology of the cultural context into an easily "read" text" (Kiernan, 1990:93). In any way, as the film represents something from life and "representation is ideological" (Gidal, 1984:25).

At the early days of cinema, its ideological aspect was surely not at front. It only throughout a certain time "developed into an ideological vehicle of unprecedented power. However massive its political and social consequences, it was the result of an over-determined convergence" (Burch, 1979:84). In 1977, Dworkin warned that "the overtones of social and political awareness, hinting the ideological proselytization of the people, by the cinema, and for a new order, that was to come" (1977:95). Then came the contemporary film theory after its chronological growing process: "the period beginning in the late 1960s and early 1970s when semiotics, structuralism, and psychoanalysis were regarded as methodological antidotes to a "soft" and unscientific humanist film criticism, and Marxist cultural critique and feminist theory were regarded as ideological antidotes to bourgeois and patriarchal aestheticism" (Sobchack, 2004:56). For some thinkers standing at the side of opposition and criticism, like Buckland "film theory (like all theory) is [nothing more than] a form of speculative thought that aims to make visible the underlying structures and absent causes that confer order and intelligibility upon films" (2009:5). Rothman, too, blames the film theory to be conflicting as it considers classical cinema only as a repressive ideological system, a system thoroughly implicated in the dominant and dominating social order" (2004:367).

The issue how ideology relates to film has been dimensioned along 60ies. "since the 1960s the prevailing tension in film theory has been between Marxism and psychoanalysis, both of which address the central issue of ideology. Psychoanalysis contributes to the theorization of a Marxian definition of ideology and in turn, this Marxian theorization itself has produced a shift in modernism" (MacDonald, 2009:35); ages-old "Look at the *cambaz*" metaphor in Turkish culture, then, was reflected by the culture industry approach by the representatives of the Frankfurt School. They had some well-placed questions to understand the relationship between film and society, and precise replies at the same time:

> What effect did the integration of film into the capitalist culture industries have on it and its audiences? As a part of mass culture, what connection was there between film aesthetics and the reproduction of the capitalist social order? How did film technology and its industrial nature inscribe within it the contradictions of capitalist society? How does fi lm and mass culture generally displace, suppress and marginalize class? What potential was there to dis-

> rupt, disturb and problematize film's relationship to capitalist socioeconomic relations? ... What mode of consumption, what kind of spectatorship would alternative film practices seek to foster? (Wayne, 2005:1-2).

Stoddart's notes on how Horkheimer and Adorno describe the 'culture industry' put a different light to the issue that might assist for a better comprehension:

> [it] is an ensemble of media forms (film, newspapers, radio) that transmits ideological representations of the world to the masses ... contemporary culture does ideological work by representing the capitalist mode of production as the only possible world, as something unchangeable. This ideological system depicts people as essentially the same, regardless of class position ... The culture industry is also a homogenizing force that renders people more alike, while promoting a false sense of individuality" ... [and according to Herbert Marcuse] "in the "one-dimensional" society of the twentieth century, capital incorporates the working classes into an ever-increasing standard of living. The expansion of scientific and technological rationality allows an ever-increasing number of people to overcome material scarcity. Through this process, elites secure the consent of subordinate groups to their unequal participation in capitalist relations of production. Where people can more easily meet their "true needs," their attention turns to the "false needs" that the capitalist classes construct. (2007:198).

"To focus on the film as a statement of ideology" (Feldmann, 1995:53), and, placing "individual films into a larger social, economic, and political context, analyzing the implicit or explicit ideology they convey" have been of the nature of the cinematic art (Gaggi, 1978:467), though it is argued that "there is no such thing as 'world cinema' ... there is, however, a great diversity of world cinemas, each with their own unique set of historical, ideological, social, cultural, industrial and economic circumstances and determinants" (Chapman, 2003:33-34). To echo the same point, Gottdiner refers a multiple thinkers (Kellner, 1989; Eagleton, 1983; Denzin, 1991; Said, 1979; Jameson, 1981; Fraser, 1989) for that they "emphasize the way systems of class, patriarchal, and racial domination are propagated through popular cultural forms, such as novels, visual images, music, or cinema" (1993:655).

To answer the question of whether ideology should definitely be sought within films, Reati quotes from Fredric James as "that under every individual text lie collective and often unconscious political readings of reality. It is the task of the critic, he asserts, to show how individual texts re-write "a prior historical or ideological 'subtext' [which] is not immediately present as such [...] but rather must itself always be (re)constructed after the fact." This means that the critic must study the works not only as individual utterances but also as part of a collective voice that emerges from their sum total (1989:24-25). While Lehman defends that "a responsible film theory and criticism curriculum will include substantial units of ideological scholarship" (1988:49), Prince claims that ideology is everywhere cinema is in concern "even in pornography" that many would not set an affiliation with ideological concern (1990:31); Robertson, in the same vein, sees a film such an ideological medium even the sound record of which may be directed for ideological targets (2006). For Green, the modification of ideologization might be simple: "'conventional ideology' may be suggested in a film 'without being overtly or didactically' [without] interfer[ing] with narrative pleasure" (1993:116). Oddly enough, Balazs was quoted where he relates the very devices of cinema, such as close-up, angle, montage, and editing—promotes a "new psychological effect" and that effect "includes contradictions, repressions, and false-consciousness," which simply opens the cinematic art fully to the field of ideologication (MacDonald, 2009:37). Even film adaptations that are mostly "seen as autonomous aesthetic works, as penetrating critical interpretations of literature," contain "ideological structures" (Sobchack, 1980:289).

A "cult of cosmopolitanism, with its accompanying disdain for the parochialism of the national," reigns in cinematic ideologization (Roberts, 1998:67). "Entertainment cinema provides surrogate satisfactions," and makes "life more bearable than it is" (Scheunemann, 2005:279-280). Popular films blind people for the unbearable sides of life, and "simply reinforce our subjection to ideology" (Smith, 1995:124). Likewise, Buckingham points out the first ring of the capitalist production chain while questing for the ideological affectivity of a [cinematic] text claiming that it "can be defined in terms of the interests it serves, which are identical with the interests of those who produce it" (1986:87). The general systems of the common capitalist production contain certain public spheres, and these public spheres "reproduce the ideological, exclusionary mechanisms of the bourgeois prototype, they also aim, for economic reasons, at a maximum of inclusion (Hansen, 1993:204), which naturally confirms the view that 'cinematic realism captures, reproduces, and communicates' 'the preexisting general cultural condition [ideology]' [by] 'absorbing an ideological message through the form of realist film narratives (Knight, 1997:41).

Ideology: Towards a Quest for Definition and Functionality

If Worland's claim that "all of Western culture is nothing less than totalitarian ideology" (1995:43) is not considered as an extremity, any kind of literary work on human sciences needs to focus on the issue of ideology. No matter a diversity of views has been witnessed ranking from an evolutionary human thought (Kinloch and Mohan, 2000:7) to that ideology does not mean much all along the complex affiliation-web of the universe but only "hardcore ideologues tend to place ideas in states of binary opposition, in "either/or" categories, even when strict logic does not dictate mutual-exclusivity" (Gaggi, 1978:462). Freeden tries a simplification to remove the turbidity declaring that "ideology is best conceived as a 'thought–action', or in more precise terms 'a form of thought–behavior that penetrates all [social and] political practice'" (Malesevic, 2006:88-89).

Hawkes dates the coining of the term ideology to 1796 that Destutt De Tracy invented the term ideology and that it meant "the science of ideas," and "originates as a 'meta-science', a science of science" (2003:59-60). The term ideology, like many other terms utilized in human sciences, does not possess a clear and consistent meaning. The term approximately refers to "systems of beliefs about human conduct" (Kinloch and Mohan, 2000:9). Williams offers three senses for a better comprehension: "1) a system of beliefs characteristic of a particular class or group; (2) a system of illusory beliefs—false ideas or false consciousness—which can be contrasted with true or scientific knowledge; and (3) the general process of meanings and ideas (1983:152-157). Van Dijk cuts short from a social point of view expressing ideology is "the basis of the social representations shared by members of a group" (1998:8), while for Culler an ideology is only "a theory" far from the possibilities of realistic practice "which justifies particular economic, political, and intellectual practices by concealing their historical origins and making them the natural components of an interpreted world" (1973:471). Robbe-Grillet and Morrisette point out an absence of innocence and good intention where they describe ideology as an "established order which is masked as natural order, which pretends to be not a creation of the society but, on the contrary, a sort of divine law dictated (1977:4). In not exactly the same but much a similar vein, Schneider sees ideology as "a cluster of ideas that rationalize some status quo or some status devoutly to be wished (1988:61). Making the issue seem to be more complicated, Neale draws a two dimensional perspective where he claims that

> Ideology, as a general concept, can be understood as comprising, on the one hand, the field of representations in discourse, a field which crosses the social formation and its practices as a whole: every practice always and necessarily involves a discursive moment; on the other hand, along with the economic and the political, ideology—the ideological—is a particular instance within a social formation, an instance comprising practices whose specific product and terrain of intervention is discursive representation and the apparatuses and institutions that specifically provide supports for these practices. (1977:18).

Ideologies are sometimes considered interestingly to be both the "systems of discursive effects organizing conflict, negotiation, and cooperation among people interacting around some institution or set of linked institutions," and "effects including beliefs and generic subject positions whereby speech, texts, and other productions are infused with import and sustenance" (Schleiner, 1999:287), which enlarges the impact sphere of the concept in the way of adding the probable "effects" of ideological motive in the scope. Nevertheless, there are denigrating assessments as well as Eagleton regards ideology "as a discursive or semiotic phenomenon," nothing more (1991:194). For Barthes ideology equals to myth (Fell, 1981:59) (Lovell, 1973:117), and ideology, "or doxa, not only forces us to produce, to speak or write in a certain way, it forces us to take sides, and compels us to choose a camp" (Watts, 2005:24). His studies "to dissect the sign systems in

Western culture were aimed "to uncover layers of ideology in capitalist societies" (Mukerji and Schudson, 1986:60). Adorno relates the concept in a rather narrowed sense with "the free market ideology of the nineteenth century," which he considers "allowed the cultural sphere a relative autonomy from the forces of production, has given way in the twentieth century to a domination of the form of exchange in all realms of social existence" (Allen, 1987:76). Post-structuralists, such as Deleuze, Guattari and Foucault, and deconstructionists, such as Derrida and his followers, ideology is "a textual or discursive construction which aims at legitimation of particular points of view that are grand narratives or foundationalist doctrines" (Lyotard 1984, 1989; Derrida 1978; Deleuze and Guattari 1977); ideology is, "operationalized within particular speech communities-it is [nothing more than] talk, image and text" (Gottdiener, 1993:656). In the field of cinematic art, Bordwell and Thompson are quoted to be asserting that ideology is a "relatively coherent system of values, beliefs, or ideas shared by some social group and often taken for granted as natural or inherently true" (Preis, 1990:18-19).

Marx and Bourgeois Ideology

Marx's basic concern of ideology is a very well-known fact: it is a mere false consciousness, which has been rather contentious. An orthodox definition of ideology that Terry Eagleton offers expands the Marxist perspective in a compact way: "ideology [is] a part of the super structure. Its function is to maintain and legitimate the "power of the social class which owns the means of economic production ... Ideology [is] shared values and ideas, taken for granted as natural and true, used to sustain the well-being of the governing powers" (Preis, 1990:18-19). On the other hand, Marx's definition of ideology related to the function of a *camera obscura*—'an upside down image in the consciousness seemed to restrict it to the abstract sphere of ideas and the mind' (Prince, 1990:31)—is highly argumentative that some even claim that definition to be just a youthful fault (Mitchell, 1987:170).

The fact that Marx goes too far by claiming that there is no text that "can be innocent of an ideological component" (Schneider, 1988:60), is weakened by regarding "only partially true" (Silberman, 1987:454). Zizek, too, does not accept that ideology is "simply a false consciousness, an illusory representation of reality (1989:15-16). It is to be sure, Marxism means the capitalist bourgeois ideology when and where the concept of ideology is in concern. The traditional Marxism defines ideology as something "generated by class society through which the dominant class comes to provide the general conceptual framework for a society's members, thus furthering the economic and political interests of that class" (Stam et al, 1992: 21-22). Calhoon, too, blames bourgeois ideology for "camouflage[ing] economic adventurousness as restraint and made restraint the touchstone of aesthetics synonymous with interiority" (Calhoon, 2000:154).

Althusser Tracing Marx: The Godfather in the Sphere of Ideology

It was the late 1960s and early 1970s when the French Marxist Louis Althusser started to have a major impact and make the study of ideology and 'the subject'. Althusser stands as a significant figure as he "stressed that ideology is grounded in institutional practices and concrete social relationships" and that "ideology was not so much ideas that imagined *themselves* independent of material circumstances but ideas that *necessarily* offered the subject an imaginary relationship to *their* real conditions of existence." The ecole called as the Althusserian criticism searched for the role of humanitarian texts in determining the position of the subject "to make sense of itself in ways that conceal contradictions within the social order, the text and by implication, the spectator" (Wayne, 2005:8-12). Althusser's formulation of ideology has been so much dominant in cinematic literature that "semiotic and psychoanalytic film theories take a cue from Althusserian formulations ... theories of subjectivity in some work evacuate Althusser's concern for the institutional loci of ideology" (Balides, 2000:141-142).

Let us remind Althusser's famous notion of 'Ideological State Apparatuses': "The State is a major educative force in this process (hegemonic dominance of the ruling class). It educates through its regulation of the life of the subordinate classes. These apparatuses reproduce class relations, and thus class subordination (the family, the school, the church and cultural institutions, as well as the law, the police and the army, the courts" (Coward, 1977:83). For Althusser "ideology represents the imaginary relationship of individuals to their real conditions of existence" (Althusser, 1971:162) (Althusser, 1970:231-233). He defines ideology as "a system of... representations (images, myths, ideas, or concepts, depending on the case) endowed with a historical existence and role within a given society" (May, 2001:55). Althusser has been reported to follow Marx "in assigning the ruling ideology the role of ensuring the submission of the workers to the ruling class." He interpreted the common official 'apparatuses' such as "the state, the church, and the military practiced control over the 'know-how' that was necessary to secure repression and ensure the viability of the existing economic system," for him, 'ideology is eternal' [because it] "exists in a material form in social practices, or in the institutions he called social apparatuses" (Freeden, 2003: 25-27).

Althusser's main thesis "that ideology constructs the subject, that the subject is an effect of ideology (Hayward, 2000:193) echoes Marx in the way that he argues "that it is in ideology (as the locus of political struggle) that men [sic] become conscious of their place in the world and in history, it is within this ideological unconsciousness that men succeed in altering the lived relation between them and the world and acquiring that new form of specific unconsciousness called ' consciousness' (Connell, 1978:133). Althusser's contribution to the argumentation about the concept of ideology has been colossal as he "provided a reason and a means for studying the sources of ideology in popular culture, to understand the fictional aspect of all consciousness, i.e. false consciousness" (Mukerji and Schudson, 1986:59). Like it happened to all the thinkers, Althusser has also been criticized. For Zhang, the Althusserian model of ideology and subjectivity remains only as "a *theoretical* hypothesis regarding the audience and the artists of socialist cinema," because "it does not explain at what juncture the subject can ignore or reject the interpellation by the dominant ideology, as did political dissidents in different times of the socialist period," and, "it does not recognize the possibility that the subject-in-subjection can and actually does negotiate and maneuver through the cracks and fissures in the ideological system and manage to 'smuggle' alternative or even subversive subtexts in socialist cinema" (2004:224). MacBean condemns Althusser to a type of narrow-mindedness by reducing all the Althusserian phenomena within a sentence of "ideology equals imaginary relations to real relations" (1972:39). Likewise, Collins accepts the Althusserian 'dictum' "that the role of ideology is to reproduce the means of production" only with a condition that it must be "applied at the level of the individual commodity" (1987:18).

Gramsci and Hegemony

An argumentation on ideology will surely be deficient if Gramsci's conceptualization of hegemony is not involved in. As Wayne points out, for Gramsci hegemony is "a force field of contestation between different groups; a dialogue even, but crucially not a dialogue between equals because capital and the capitalist state have awesomely more resources at their disposal to shape the agenda and implement policies and practical changes (2005:5-6), which is either directly or indirectly connected with the issue of ideology. While Mukerji stresses upon the political aspect and claims that Gramsci is "much more concerned with the political functioning of ideology" and "hegemony is achieved in large part through the use of ideology" (1986:59), Harpole underlines the link between the concept of film and Gramsci's 'ideological hegemony' as that Gramsci's approach is described by several elements such as "the beliefs, values, cultural traditions, and myths which create a consensus that perpetuates the status quo." (1980:22).

Foucault, Logocentrism, and Other Prospects

In contrast to "the earlier theoretical formation urged political critiques of ideology within Marxist framework, more recent reception-based studies appear more consistent with a dispersed (often implicitly Foucauldian) field of subcultural identities, agendas and resistance" (Durant, 2000:10). Foucault who is reported to be "less interested in subjectivity," and rather "focuses on institutional practices and discourses" (Balides, 1993:26), considers the notion of ideology rather problematic as "it always stands in virtual opposition to something else which is supposed to count as truth'; it 'necessarily' refers 'to something of the order of the subject'; and [it] stands in a 'secondary position relative to something which functions as its infrastructure, as its material, economic determinant" (Foucault, 1980:118).

So, how will ideology work in the postmodern sense? Logocentrism is presented as a concept offering an insight into the issue, as "all grand narratives require a hierarchical mode of representation and constitute a form of logocentrism;" that is, "in logocentric representation a set of concepts or beliefs are chosen as the fundamental referents which become the focus of the argument ... Once constructed in discourse, the pyramid of representation, which privileges particular ideas at the expense of others, can be invoked simply by referring to one central concept, which then sets off the chain of associations constructed by the ideology (Gottdiener, 1993:656). Mystifying the puzzle, Kracauer argues that "new forms of ideology" are produced by "the psychosexual dynamics of consumption" (Hansen, 1992:66), while Eisenstadt points out the eminent role of complex web of relations in modern life "shifts in the principles of legitimation, the symbols and the boundaries of traditional community, together with a change in the composition of the ruling elites, were connected with the ideological restructuring of the new center-periphery relations towards modernity" (İrem, 2002:96).

It has also been observed that the approach to ideology has involved shifts in two different dimensions:

> Change occurred in the content or thrust of ideological critique, from concern with the way the capitalist class controlled the workers struggle through ideas to a general interest in the way all hegemonic interests use culture to dominate others. On the other hand, change occurred in the mechanism believed to underlie the effect of ideology, from the propagation of beliefs manifested as control of thought or consciousness to the encoding of hegemonic ideas through language, visual images and texts. We are prone to be victims of ideology not because our minds are controlled but because we use common but biased images and figures of speech that are

> provided by society or its major texts. Our manipulation by particular, powerful interests involves the domination of desires, 656-consumer choices, political preferences, belief systems, academic knowledge and other symbolic representations, rather than some specific effect directed at ideas about the putative performance of the economy. (Gottdiener, 1993:655-656)

The very meaning and definition of ideology has been an issue of argumentation. For example, Prince claims that ideology "should be treated as a phenomenon accessible to observation and verification, explicable through a diverse range of methodologies, if [it] is to be more than a set of abstract ideas or social values" (Prince, 1990:40). Mas'ud Zavarzadeh also argues that "the self-absorbed pleasures of contemporary theory affected a shift in the meaning of 'ideology,' 'power,' and 'hegemony' which turned them into abstractions detached from a materialist analysis of social class (Dittmar, 1995:39). Balkin, on the other hand, prefers a bidirectional approach while urging to draw the frame of ideology: "[it is] simultaneously "empowering, useful and adaptive on the one hand, and disempowering, distorting and maladaptive on the other" (1998:126).

The more complete the world as appearance,
the more impenetrable the appearance of ideology.

Theodor W. Adorno (Silberman, 1987:456)

Ideology and Art: Two Cognitive Aludels

Buckingham poses two crucial questions that have still been anticipating replies: "to what extent can the identification of ideology be seen as a process of unmasking or exposing the underlying values of a text? Is ideology something *inherent* in texts?" (1986:82). As an effort to seek an answer we can glance at the phrase of 'ideology of representation'. The mere existence of the concept of 'ideology of representation' alone has been the competent evidence of how much ideology and art have been interlaced, if art is handled to be a text—a way and form of representation—far from Staiger's definition of that art is "a discourse within a particular conjunction-for the purpose of women's cinema, the bourgeois, sexist ideology of male dominated capitalism" (Staiger, 1985:16). Following a moderate sensitivity, Mitchell argues that "the connections between art and ideology are neither accidental, nor (at least, not necessarily) direct" (Mitchell, 1971:152), whereas Brecht boasts as "one could never escape ideology" (Shattuc, 1993:40). Kracauer, too, "equated ideology with art, arguing that, because art emphasized the transformation of the world through the use of conventions and formulas" (Aitken, 1998:130). Lovell's two-sided conceptualization of ideology is not to be ignored:

> The concept of ideology points two ways; to the cultural artefacts and behaviors within which it is embedded, and whose own spe-

> cific structural organization has to be understood if we are to ' read ' them correctly; and to society and the social groups whose ideology they are, and in relation to whose situation the artefacts have ideological meaning. (1973:121).

Beyond any doubt, ideology and visuality have been married for a long time as Freeden indicates that "throughout history ideologies have been transmitted through visual and pictorial forms" (2003:114). The same opinion is echoed by Volosinov as that "the domain of ideology coincides with the domain of signs ... Wherever a sign is present, ideology is present too" (1996:468). The relation between textual signification and ideology is clarified by Eagleton as that "the text is neither an epiphenomenon of ideology nor a wholly autonomous element. The 'truth' of the text is not an essence but a practice—the practice of its relation to ideology and in terms of that to history" (Eagleton, 1978:98) (Stoneman, 1979:49). However, "the ideological significance of any text—or any genre—is always to be sought in a context-specific analysis" (Neale, 1990:65). The essential motive is embedded "between different types of reading of the same textual material on the basis of ideological positioning (dominant, negotiated and oppositional readings) forced a corresponding wedge between texts and the subject positions they might be thought to prescribe" (Durant, 2000:9).

The fact that Marx refers to ideology as "inversion of real relations like that inversion in the *camera obscura* from positive to negative," and "recognizes 'that seeing is not merely a capturing of the world, an imprinting of meaning within an image' (Polan, 1982:134) attracts the attentions to the role of art that is too much related to 'seeing' and 'image. Whereas Gaggi finds "Marxist oriented critics" rather obsessive since they "wish to emphasize the role of ideology (implicit or explicit) in all art and to reject the notion that any art work can be an unbiased, non-ideological reflection of reality" (Gaggi, 1978:462), what Barthes said in 70s on the impact of the bourgeois ideology might not be underestimated regarding the reciprocal positions of ideology and art: "Our press, our films, our theater, our popular literature, our rituals, our justice . . . the cooking we dream of, the clothes we wear, everything in everyday life is dependent on the representation which the bourgeoisie has and makes us have of the relations between man and the world" (1970:227). Barthes was quite decisive on the issue; for him "any theory of writing. . .must include a concept of ideology" (Rosen, 1981:17); and as all the forms of art include somehow a way of writing, art can in no way be conceptualized free of ideology. On the other side, the "potential to exhibit ideology is characteristic of the aesthetic process" (Kuntzel, 1973:49), and, we have been witnessing "the historically changing relationship between aesthetics and ideology (Allen, 1987:238), which directly or indirectly brings about that "narrative form exposes the fissures within ideology (Brown, 1998:176); no matter "authentic art [that is mostly considered to be safeguarded against ideological associations] always transcends the ideological limits of its time, yielding us insight into the realities which ideology hides from view" (Eagleton, 1976:18).

According to the notorious "mechanistic Marxist conception," "art and ideology are equivalent" (Kuntzel, 1973:49). MacBean and Roy blaze their Marxism when they relate the way in which art is produced to "the class struggle, and, "art is useful to the ruling class as an ideological tool which disseminates values (e.g., contemplation rather than action) that serve to perpetuate ruling class power and privilege-such considerations of use value are taboo" (1972:32). Althusser, another well-known Marxist, is quoted as tracing the classical mentality: "What art makes us *see,* and therefore gives us in the forms of "*perceiving*" and "*feeling*"... is the ideology from which it is born, in which it bathes, from which it detaches itself as art, and to which it alludes" (Klinger, 1984:31). For Knight, the concept of 'ideological product' was created by the movement of second semiology (1993:322) that was somehow related to the 'myth of success' indicated by "Adorno's characterization of the reception of the product of the culture industry as "mass deception" (Waldman, 1977:60). It is then the ideology of culture industry that "attempts to manipulate the masses; the ideology of the culture industry itself becomes as internally antagonistic as the very society which it aims to control (Adorno and Levin, 1982:202). That is, "the pleasures of mass culture ... must be reassuring pleasures that support the racism, sexism, and class oppression of bourgeois ideology ... [and] that "cover over" a serious ideological complicity, a false consciousness (Rutsky, 1990:12-14). "Visual images," produced in a particular cultural milieu, indeed, "in and of themselves," are [innocently] free from ideology and that it is their cultural work, their production of meaning, that serves various ideological purposes" (Reynolds, 1997:392) while "ideology is necessarily [not] uniform and coherent throughout a culture (Saxton, 1986:22). Walsh's psychoanalytic analysis on ideological discourses in modern cultures is rather impressive: "the imaginary is defined as an area of plenitude and unity in which both ideological discourses and discourses of desire operate' ... within the Imaginary the personal (desire) is channeled to the collective (ideology) through the intervening agency of discourse" (1996:9). MacCabe puts all the blame of ideological production on the individual artist without taking the external conditions into the account where he philosophies that "ideology is produced ... in so far as the artist is able to grasp and articulate the social changes taking place within the world of individuals and feelings" (1976:24).

Cinema is one of the languages through which the world communicates itself to itself. They constitute its ideology for they reproduce the world as it is experienced when filtered through the ideology.

(Comolli and Narboni, 1971:30)

Ideology and Cinema: A Never-ending Story of Two Coats of Paint

Chapman displays one of the basic realities of cinematic art: "while films may not directly reflect society, they nevertheless are informed by and respond to the societies and circumstances in which they were produced," which gains its fullest meaning by the fact that films maintain at their roots an ideologically normative regulatory function as "the semiotics of film itself is ideological" (Henderson, 1975:20). "By placing a film within multifarious intertextual and historical frames," Klinger argues, "the film's variable, even contradictory, ideological meanings come into focus" (1997:110). If so, where does ideology fit into a discussion of cinema? For Aronowitz, it is the particular "film [itself that] generates its own ideology; its way of seeing constitutes technically its ideological parameters" (1979:117). In this way, "the middle voice of film narration [becomes] the voice of ideology" (Kavanagh, 1979:58). The way Hayward relates cinema to ideology, indeed, seems to be a much more satisfactory reply to this crucial question:

> Cinema is an ideological apparatus by nature of its very seamlessness. We do not see how it produces meaning—it renders it invisible, naturalizes it ... Social reality does not present easy solutions, life is not 'order/disorder/order restored' as the classic narrative would have us believe. But because of the reality-effect which seamlessness produces, the spectator is easily stitched into the

> narrative, the process of recognition and identification is under way and so too the ideological function of film—which is why generic repetition works so well and we go back again and again to the movies. (2000:194).

Zizek's approach to ideology in relation to cinema does not differ much. He argues that "especially in the cinema, we always have ideology-as-fantasy-frame underpinning, as well as placing ideology-as-discourse" (Elsaesser, 2005:347). For Zizek, cinema does whatever ideologically it does via phantasy: "A fantasy is simultaneously pacifying, disarming (providing an imaginary scenario which enables us to endure the abyss of the Other's desire) *and* shattering, disturbing, unassimilable into our reality" (McGowan, 2007:38). Hayward indicates Baudry as "the first film theorists to suggest that the cinematic apparatus or technology has an ideological effect upon the spectator," Baudry in sum claimed:

> In the simplest instance the cinematic apparatus purports to set before the eye and ear realistic images and sounds. However, the technology disguises how that reality is put together frame by frame. It also provides the illusion of perspectival space. This double illusion conceals the work that goes into the production of meaning and in so doing presents as natural what in fact is an ideological construction, that is, an idealistic reality. (2000:15).

Elsaesser claimed that every single film somehow includes ideology simply because each film has a narration; and the techniques of narration are not exempt from ideology (1975:14) (Balides, 1993:36). Baudrillard, focuses on a similar point when he utters that "the contemporary subject negotiates cinematic logics which are perpetual and kinetic, organized by an open-ended, serial displacement of images, which simulate basic epistemological categories, including "real" and "unreal" and "experience" and "ideology" (Downing and Bazargan, 1991:85). As "the final [cinematic] product always remains under the control of the studio and its dominant financial and ideological drives" (O'Flinn, 1999:81-82), it becomes impossible to get rid of ideology in cinematic art (Jones-Thomson, 2008:88), and cinema in this way serves to the naturalization processes of the dominant ideology (Simpson,

1993:5-6). Let us give an ear to the voice of Comolli and Narboni, which time has not been able to make wither away:

> The *majority* of films in all categories are the unconscious instruments of the ideology which produces them ... For all films are commodities and therefore objects of trade, even those whose discourse is explicitly political ... This merging of ideology and film is reflected in the first instance by the fact that audience demand and economic response have also been reduced to one and the same thing. In direct continuity with political practice, ideological practice reformulates the social need and backs it up with a discourse. This is not a hypothesis, but a scientifically-established fact. The ideology is talking to itself; it has all the answers ready before it asks the questions. Certainly there is such a thing as public demand, but ' what the public wants ' means ' what the dominant ideology wants '. The notion of a public and its tastes was created by the ideology to justify and perpetuate itself. And this public can only express itself via the thought-patterns of the ideology. The whole thing is a closed circuit, endlessly repeating the same illusion. (1971:31).

Mulvey, the well-known feminist author, points out the ideological aspect of the cinematic art regarding the ideology centered on gender differentiation where she points out that "a new mode of making and interpreting films is necessary because film audiences—both male and female—view cinematic images through a male gaze, unconsciously identifying with a (white) heterosexual, male perspective and conforming to the patriarchal ideology that defines classical narrative films and acts to objectify women" (Christian, 2011:995). Marxism, in the most general sense, has a common point with the cinematic art: "they are both interested in the masses ... the social reach of film explains the theoretical and practical interest that Marxists have shown towards the medium" (Wayne, 2005:1). When ideology intervenes, almost all elements of a film transform into something else, as Zhang argues and exemplifies: "a discussion of contrastive characteristics of pre-socialist and socialist cinemas can help delineate the radical process whereby the latter replaced the former in a matter of years" (Zhang, 2004:202):

Aspect	***Socialist cinema***	***Pre-socialist cinema***
Ideology	class consciousness	Confucian or bourgeois virtues
Heroes	workers, peasants, soldiers	petit-bourgeois intellectuals
Setting	factories, mines, villages, camps	domestic, private, personal spaces
Action	violent struggle	sentimental persuasion
Concern	public welfare, collective interest	personal frustration
Process	identification with the masses	individual fulfillment
Method	typification (good and bad)	ambivalence (middle characters)
Goal	political correctness (Party-state)	humanism (nation-people)

When filmic ideology is in concern sequelisation is at work, it is "played out and employed to serve specific ideological and industrial imperatives (Jess-Cooke, 2009:70). Friedman openly claims that "a film is an ideological expression" (1984:513) since "film internalizes industrial movement and manifests it as (a form of) consciousness" (Beller, 1995:179), which automatically brings about an "epistemological repression" (Johnson, 1979:32) that is paraphrased by MacBean, "who believes that the most significant function of any movie is its role as a conveyor of ideology" (Gaggi, 1978:462). Metz, an eminent authority in film studies, claims "that the feature film ideologically equates the spectator with the narrating agent" (Cooper, 2002:155) (Cooper, 1998:107) (Guzzetti, 1973:306-307), while he seems to be tracing MacBean when he philosophizes as "realistic" films do not present reality but a specific notion of reality" (Gaggi, 1978:468) (Metz and Guzzetti 1976:75) (Eaton, 1976:116) (Williams, 1971:21) (Willemen, 1972:38) (Greene, 1974:137) (Allen, 1993:21) (Gallie, 1972:135) (Carroll, 1985:80) (Staiger, 1985:15), which constructs the fundamental infrastructure of the ideological motive in cinematic art. In sum, there are two ideological attitudes for Metz whenever reality in cinematic art is in concern: "*cinema direct* (the ideology of the objective recording of external reality) and *cinema verite* (the ideology of the redeeming intervention)" (Cegarra, 1973:151). Bordwell and Jean-Louis Comolli, in the same way, relate film ideology as "a continuation of earlier varieties of realism" and "reproducing reality" (Cooper, 2002:143).

In addition to that game-of-reality, Adorno and Levin underline that film provides models for collective behavior should surely be regarded as "an additional imposition of ideology" presented by the cinematic art (1982:203). Barthes, on the other hand, sees cinema as "a grand metaphor for the very submission of self to system: "ideology is, in effect, the imaginary of an epoch, the cinema of a society," he suggests somehow "that we can no longer even understand ideological practices; we are either totally inside them, caught up phenomenologically in ideology's flow, or outside them" (Polan, 1981:43-44). Still, he emphasizes on that "cinema participates in the "ideological abuse" of bourgeois culture," in the same way that "ideology ... forces us to take sides, and compels us to choose a camp" (Watts, 2005:22-24). It is a widely known fact that contemporary film theorists generally claim that film is inherently a discourse of capitalist ideology, and they base this this claim upon 'Saussurean linguistics' (Buckland, 1989:82). As Poague writes, "much cine-semiotics operates on the Saussurean assumption that linguistic meaning is arbitrarily and ideologically coded, that film meaning is similarly constrained and determined, hence that the social function of the "cinematic apparatus" is to impose "bourgeois" language and its value system on the film audience" (1985:26).

Eisenstein oracled once as that "cinematography will be genetically ideological (Michelson, 1976:29) signaling the vital place of montage "which plays a decisive role in the strategy of the ideology produced" (Baudry and Williams, 1974:42) though there are numerous ways in which films can (re)produce the/an ideology, "a number of styles are 'open' for use" (Gidal, 1984:26). That is, instead of an obsession with the mechanisms of receiving and spectatorship, one should keep in mind that "filming mechanism [is] an ideological machine that could be representative factor of ideology" (Baudry and Williams, 1974:44) (Cooper, 2002:152). It is to be sure that "the cinematic apparatus is ideologically not neutral" (MacCabe, 1976:8), which unfortunately leads many people to the mistake pointed out by Bordwell:

> many may regard as the most extraordinary feature of the text, that its treatment of the role of ideology within the occupational

> confines of the film-making community (Hollywood) is confined to an examination of various 'recipe' texts, technical specifications and the like, that debate or prescribe how to deliver or render a narrative, an image, without exhibiting a great deal of curiosity about the social or political values of what is rendered. (1988:82).

The first offer to utilize cinema in an ideological way is dated back to Ivan von Bloch's 'Peace Project' in 1898 (Halachmi, 1998:94-96). Likewise, the historical turning points of film criticism have been classified in three periods: "the pre-academic moment of cine-clubs by the avant-gardists during the 1920s and later by the Cahiers du cinéma critics during the 1950s; the academic moment of post-'68 'Screen Theory'; and the post-theory moment of the return to history" (Hudson and Zimmerman, 2009:136). It was 1970s that the notion the cinema was considered to be a vehicle for transferring a specific ideology basically dominated the debates in film studies. It started in France, there were "two avant-garde cinema groups-the Dziga Vertov group and the Cinéthique group ... they were strongly influenced by Althusserian Marxism (mainly on the issue of the ideological apparatus of the State), by Lenin's analysis of the transformation of capitalism into imperialism, and by the philosophical writings of Mao Tse Tung" (Scheunemann, 2005:273-274). By the mid-1970s the concept of "the unconscious ideology of spectators" started to be discussed in the circles of cinematography (Andrew, 2000:343). There appeared two journals—for some, two ecoles—*Screen* and *Cahiers De Cinema*. The Screen school mainly argued that "the cinema is a tool of the ruling (bourgeois) class because it "naturally" centers passive viewers before a spectacle, giving them the illusion of mastery while in fact chaining them in position as subjects of an ideology that stabilizes the socio-economic and political order" (Bazin, 2005). History in the course of time witnessed 1970's theories of spectatorship: "they emerged at the threshold of a paradigmatic transformation of the ways films are disseminated and consumed. In other words, even as these theories set out to unmask the ideological effects of the classical Hollywood cinema, they might effectively, and perhaps unwittingly, have mummified the spectator-subject of classical cinema" (Hansen, 1993:198) which also was the first blaze of the Screen Theory that

> a group of left-leaning humanities scholars developed in the pages of Screen a dizzying and influential blend of Marxism, psychoanalysis and semiotics that ultimately positioned mainstream cinema as an 'ideological apparatus'. Louis Althusser, Antonio Gramsci and Bertolt Brecht frequently bumped into each other on the pages of the journal ... Althusser's rethinking of the Marxist thesis of economic determination was particularly important. In work throughout the 1960s and 1970s, Althusser had argued that 'superstructures' (legal/political and ideological practices) had a greater effect on the social formation than previous Marxist scholarship had suggested, even if the economy determined that formation 'in the last instance'. Althusser's work increasingly utilized psychoanalysis to explain how ideology shapes or 'authors' subjectivity. To do so, he drew in particular on Jacques Lacan's structuralist reworking of Freud to propose that ideology 'interpellates'—that is, addresses, appeals to—an individual as a free and unified subject, but that this position is an 'imaginary' one, masking the 'real conditions of existence' ... Lacan supplied, for Althusser and many others in his wake, what seemed to be an elucidation of the recognition/misrecognition structures associated with ideology. The connections drawn between ideology and the Unconscious shaped the development of a Screen Theory that focused on the question of the spectator, conceived as a textually implicated subject. (Grieveson, 2009:182-183).

The ideology understanding of *Screen* was essentially based on Althusser at first; then Lacan and psychoanalysis also involved in (Coward, 1977:77). "A number of questions around realism, ideology and the placing of spectator in relation to film system" Kuhn notes, "have been central concerns of Screen (1977:124). Three of the best-known essays from *Screen* published in the mid-seventies have impressed the cinematic art:

> Colin MacCabe's "Realism and Cinema: Notes on Some Brechtian Theses," Laura Mulvey's "Visual Pleasure and Narrative Cinema," and Stephen Heath's "Narrative Space." All three were deeply indebted to "Cinema/Ideology/Criticism," the 1968 Cahiers du Cinema editorial by Pierre Narboni and Jean-Louis Comolli; all three were suspicious of narrative and popular pleasure; all three subsumed individual practices under generalized formal categories, which in turn were assigned ideological effects; all three described the way a

hypostasized "subject" was positioned in the filmic text; and all three deconstructed classic realism, implicitly arguing for a modernist or avant-garde cinema that would fragment identity and identification, decentering the character, the reader, and the author. (Naremore, 1990:20).

For Casetti, the theory "exhausted itself" throughout the course of time because "it fell victim to its own rigidity and repetition ... during the 1990s, it became clear that ... it was not able ... to provide responses to the questions which began to be posed" (Buckland, 2009:3). During the period the theory was dominant, "the styles of film-making grounded in perceptual realism, or "naturalism," were frequently criticized on the grounds of a presumed capacity to "naturalize" ideology" (Aitken, 2009:328).

The ideological cinema comments started to be published in *Cahiers Du Cinema* in 60s with Brect. It was Brect who "called the 'apparatus' or 'public entertainment machine', the social and economic conditions in which art is socially produced" (Hillier, 1986:9). It was as early as "after 1968," and it was "*Cahiers*" that "made a first attempt to introduce ideology into the debate in its exploration of Hollywood films that either 'resisted' or reflected dominant ideology" (Hayward, 2000:25). Still, it was *Cahiers* that "developed a criticism explicitly orientated to ideology critique ... offered a typology of the different relations that could occur between film texts and ideology" (Wayne, 2005:13) (Darke, 1993:364) (Fletcher, 1988:3) (Rutsky, 1990:5). Jean-Louis Comolli was the name under most of the work in this issue. He penned a series of articles in *Cahiers Du Cinema* attempting to "re-read the idealist discourse from the standpoint of the main area it represses—the economic, political, and ideological" in order to begin to write a history of the cinema from the point of view of historical and dialectical materialism" (Waldman, 1977:51). The following quotation from the text published in 1971 that defines film and cinema brings the intellectual stance of the journal fully to light:

> What is a film? On the one hand it is a particular product, manufactured within a given system of economic relations, and involving labour ... to produce ... assembling a certain number of workers for

> this purpose... It becomes transformed into a commodity, possessing exchange value, which is realized by the sale of tickets and contracts, and governed by the laws of the market. On the other hand, as a result of being a material product of the system, it is also an ideological product of the system, which in France means capitalism ... .Because every film is part of the economic system it is also a part of the ideological system, for 'cinema ' and ' art' are branches of ideology ... every film is political, inasmuch as it is determined by the ideology which produces it ... The cinema is all the more thoroughly and completely determined because unlike other arts or ideological systems its very manufacture mobilizes powerful economic forces in a way that the production of literature ... Clearly, the cinema 'reproduces' reality: this is what a camera and film stock are for—so says the ideology. But the tools and techniques of film-making are a part of 'reality' themselves, and furthermore 'reality' is nothing but an expression of the prevailing ideology. Seen in this light, the classic theory of cinema that the camera is an impartial instrument which grasps, or rather is impregnated by, the world in its 'concrete reality' is an eminently reactionary one. What the camera in fact registers is the vague, unformulated, untheorized, unthought-out world of the dominant ideology. (Comolli and Narboni, 1971:29-30).

For the Frankfurt School, the panorama seems to be rather pessimistic and not much different from the frame drawn by *Screen* and *Cahiers Du Cinema*:

> the sinister role of capitalism extends beyond merely dumping unwanted goods on a hapless public. Itself the ultimate expression of capitalism, the entertainment industry seeks to provide an ideological justification for capitalism, to help make the system as a whole function and sustain its power over the masses. To accomplish this purpose, as the Frankfurt school understands it, the entertainment industry must reconcile the masses to the system that exploits them and, thus, prevent them from even thinking about rebelling against it. With this end in view, Hollywood creates a mass cultural myth of hope, tantalizing the American people with the prospect of bettering their lives and escaping from their downtrodden condition. Hollywood manufactures a picture of society as a kind of giant lottery in which anyone can win the big payoff. The

> vast majority of individuals in the capitalist system may have to live with being exploited and accept their passive roles as losers, but, if they can be bombarded with striking images of winners, of people who have been lucky enough to beat the system, they can live on in hope that they too might someday cash in on good fortune and join the magic circle of the successful. Horkheimer and Adorno see that the culmination of this image of society as a lottery is the myth of success in Hollywood itself. (Cantor, 2006:146-147) (Hunt and Wing-Fai, 2008:73-74).

It is the 'iconicity' of films that gives birth to the 'ideological complicity' of the cinematic art "because it allows the filmic image to function as an advertisement for the world "as is." (Hansen, 1992:45). Adorno develops the same argument somewhere else philosophizing that "mass-cultural hieroglyphics actually spell out a behavioral script; by disguising the very fact that they were written, and with it their heteronomous origin, they create the regressive illusion of a common discourse." That is, "similar to film theorists of the 1970s such as Metz and Baudry," he "ascribes this ideological effect to the configuration of the apparatus [and] the psychotechnical conditions of film reception" (Hansen, 1992:47). Here Althusser's idea that "cinema as an institution performs an ideological function" comes forth once more (Althusser, 1971). As Green notes, "we, as cultural consumers, are again interpellated as "citizens" of (subjects in) this harmonious world; not only is our cultural milieu structured so as to reward passive consumption, but we are also assured that there is ultimately nothing to be active about (Green, 1993:102-104). By this way, "the cinema serves only to mask the effects of ideology" which guides us to the fact that "we need to understand the medium's resourcefulness in using cinematography to inscribe ideology and politics" (Dittmar, 1995:40).

All of this complications make us be attracted to the technical elements of cinema that give way the possibility of making films ideological units: "since the effect of seamlessness, the absence of a visible author, and the very womblike nature of film projection make of film a cultural form that strikes at and activates our deepest fantasies, this would appear to be the core source of whatever ideological messages we ultimately derive from cinema as an institution" (Green, 1993:120). Instead of a clear openness, ideology becomes embedded in cinema as ideology "eliminates the distance between ideas and reality and also reproduces those constantly in films" (MacDonald, 2009:37). The fact that "the cinema can thus appear as a sort of psychic apparatus of substitution, corresponding to the model defined by the dominant ideology" (Baudry and Williams, 1974:46) causes in that "cinema's ideological practice is determined by the same strategy of authority" (Abbott, 1979:14). At the end of this high complicated process, the point to be reached is not far from that "the conception of cinema as an ideological practice entails consideration of the ways in which that practice is situated and relayed in institutions (places, organizations, sets of practices) in which part of the material work of ideology goes forward" (Abbott, 1979:50). Prince determines the base of problem as "the implication of discursive equivalence, the idea that all cinematic representations are, in the end, equally artificial, since all are the constructions of form or ideology" (1996:35). He then offers the challenge for film theory: "to find a method of conceptualizing the presence and place of ideology within cultural products that does not result in a unidirectional communicational process, flattening and rendering passive spectatorial activity" (Prince, 1988:30). As "cinema participates in the "ideological abuse" of bourgeois culture" (Watts, 2005:22), and "audiences accustomed to bourgeois movies which emphasize entertainment or "art" are certainly not going to dig hearing lengthy analyses of revisionism or of ideology or of the need to struggle against bourgeois individualism" (MacBean and Roy, 1972:33), ideology always find a way to keep itself in dark. The very fact that "cinema is conceived as pure spectacle" (Chanan, 1997:375) also contributes much to this widespread attitude.

Though less in number, there have been some voices opposing to that ideology has an undeniable impact on the cinematographic art. Ferenz considers the belief that film spectators are "passive" receivers and that any given film "railroads" them into "identifying" with the "ideology" of that film" rather "problematic and, eventually, self-defeating as it is popular" (2009:282). Martin even gets angry at that "every individual character in a film—of a particular gender, sexual orientation, color, nationality or age—is taken as a representative of their entire class" (2000:12). Carroll notes that "film is primarily a resource rather than a source of ideology," [while he has] "no reason to assert dogmatically that a film could never invent ideology" (1990:359). Likewise, he is quoted somewhere else "[to reject] the notion that the cinema engages the spectator on an unconscious level ... and that classical films (or mass entertainment movies) are inherently discourses of capitalist ideology" (Buckland, 1989:82).

Under the light shed by authors above, it might be asserted that cinema resembles to a double-edged sword, which evokes mostly fear rather than relief, peace, hope and reliance. The most alarming feature of it stands out that it can simply be activated as an agent of political and ideological manipulation and cultural colonialism. Besides, that it might be utilized as an agent of cultural militancy and political/ideological revolutions, as exemplified dozens of time throughout history, puts a dark shadow upon its artistic and aesthetic aspects.

Turkish Cinema: Lingering around the Limbo of Non/Existence

Cinema on the Last Days of the Ottoman Magnificence

For almost thirty decades, Turkey and her people have been suffering from a fatal conflict of identity: to stay as conservatives or to become modernists. No single field of humanitarian sciences will be scoped elaborately and precisely in case this conflict is neglected if it is Turkey that is in concern. The worse than the existence of the conflict, it has been impressive on the destiny of the country and its people for so long, in this or that way. For Karpat this conflict "weakened the energy and production capacity possessed by society and narrowed the scope of the reforms," and, "as players taking place in this conflict, leaders heading the conservatives were not people with open ideas and intellects; they opposed all innovations. Modernists completely rejected the old order. In conclusion, these two extremes started to feel an increasing hatred towards each other" (2011: 181-182). Unlike the rest of the world, in the history of Turkey, ideologies "originated due to rehabilitating the administrative system," and have [had] characteristics that are devoid of real ideological fundamentals" (Karpat, 2004:25-26).

At the beginning of the 20th Century, it was much worse. There were three main ideological currents debated in the Empire: The Turkist, the Islamist, and the Westernist. Their attitudes towards modernization were in a deep conflict: "The Islamists rejected and opposed modernization and although the Westernists and the Turkists agreed on the necessity for drastic change they disagreed upon the extent to which Western institutions should be adopted and upon the role that Islam should play within the society. The Westernists advocated total acceptance of European values, culture, and technology and favored a secular state" (Szyliowicz, 1970:151). The sad as much as pathetic story of westernization dominated the fate of the country. Long before and after the heavy defeat of the World War I, "the West has been the inspiration, often the motivator, behind the efforts undertaken by the Ottoman rulers to modernize their state ... The assumption was that the Turks could, should and would become members of the civilized western world (Kushner, 1997:230-231). For Göle all the blame was upon the currents of secularism and positivism as they were "the two pillars of the Turkish modernization experience that began in the 19th Century and reached its institutional and ideological peak in 1923 ... Rather than Anglo-Saxon liberalism, French Jacobinism, with its highly centralized model of change, became the prototype for reform of Turkish modernists. Hence, secularization itself became part of that process of social engineering rather than an outcome of the process of modernization and societal development" (Göle, 1997a:48). Tragic enough, the intellectual, political and academic agendas have still been engaged with similar debates no matter all the word has entered a new millennium.

As of the cinematographic art, the panorama was not/ has not been in much difference: the "traumatic identity crisis that [Turkey and her people] have been stuck in for a long time as a nation, has been one of the reasons why [Turkish people] are not in a place [they] deserve as in many branches of art and why [they] cannot put our stamp on the silver screen as it deserves (Acar, 2010:48). Baş summarizes the problem in short: there is an identity problem in Turkish cinema," which is of no surprise as the work of art of a country does surely generate from the very essential/national culture of her people. If the "national 'self-portraits' as depicted in large-scale exhibitions ... are ... embodiments of reflexive as well as nonreflexive routine enactions of 'national identities'" (Malesevic, 2006:51), then, it should be deduced how deeply the cinematographic art of a particular country is connected with the national identity of her people.

It must have been the result of that conflict and identity crisis that the "statesmen in our country [Turkey] did not like the cinema in general. Cinema started first in the palace, but with the onset of the Republic cinema was not appreciated too much ... cinema was not regarded as a need in those days, no benefit was expected from the cinema or maybe it was feared that "it might be an uncontrollable art form" (Güneş, 2010:61). Indeed, it is not too much surprising that those who did not have to deal with such a conflict or crisis welcomed the art of cinema: "during the time when the show was made, Pera was the location of the non-moslem citizens and Istanbul society. Thus, after the entrance of cinema into our country [Turkey], this segment had taken over this new art" (Hazar, 2010:171). That is, "the fact that cinema has entered through non-moslem districts such as Kadiköy and Beyoglu into Istanbul and that all of the film producers and cinema operators were non-moslem Ottoman citizens and those with foreign nationalities caused the public to keep its distance from the cinema" (Enderun, 2011:18).

Enver Pasha, who witnessed that the countries which participated in World War I used cinema as a weapon ordered to found an institution of cinema that was directed by the army as in Germany. The Agency of Central Military Cinema was established in 1915. This agency filmed a number of "movies related with war, or lives of sultan and chief commander" (Özuyar, 2011:65). As destiny would have it, the agency that had been founded for propaganda served to the art of cinema more than the army. The army cinema acted in this area sometimes as a producer, sometimes with director officers and sometimes by providing materials and troops. Özuyar points out that cinema was deemed an instrument of entertainment for Ottomans, when it entered the Yildiz Palace during the reign of Abdülhamit II, "through the efforts of Bertrand of French origin, who was one of the senior magicians of the palace" (2011:20). For whatever aim and in whichever way the cinema entered the lives of Ottoman Turks, there is a pinching truth about the cinema of those days: "cinema in our country [Turkey] was produced and shown in a manner that was far from a domestic approach" (Hazar, 2010:177). On those days, it was 'the Young Turks' who became prominent in leading the destiny of the country so much that "the most important and undoubtedly the most fateful period in Ottoman history is the Young Turk or Union and Progress era in 1908-18." It was again the Young Turks who "were the first group in the Ottoman state to approach the social, political, and cultural transformation of their society in the spirit of modern politics (Karpat, 1975:276). Due to this fact, they deserve a massive attention as "many of the ideas put forward during the Republican period were actually formulated in 1908 [by these people]" (Karpat, 2011:248).

The Single-Party Period till 1950, the Beginning of the Multi-Party Democracy

This era starts with the republican legislature, the Grand National Assembly which was founded on April 23, 1920 during a war of independence. The fact that "the parliaments of the early twenties found themselves confronted with the issues of a transition ... from a religious monarchy based on land tenure and military organization to a Western-style, secular, republican political system" (Kalaycıoğlu, 1980:125) was the essential concept of the era which witnessed "the foundation of the new elitist order created by the Young Turk Revolution," [that had been] established upon the "socio-political foundations prepared in the Young Turks period" (Karpat, 2011:17-18). The efforts of republican reformists aimed "to bring the national Turkish culture instead of the Islam culture they wished to eradicate," "to eliminate traditionalists and gain control of the Grand National Assembly and apply their own reform programs," and, "secularism has turned increasingly into the most important principle" (Karpat, 2011:26, 29,30). The intellectual background of the founders of the Republic was totally impacted by varying derivations of materialism: "the positivistic theory of Auguste Comte, the physiologist trend of Claude Bernard, the evolution theory of Charles Darwin and the biological materialism of Ludwig Buchner" (Demir, 2004:60), "opposition to spiritualism, scientology ... authoritarianism, intellectual elitism, social Darwinism and nationalism, were first transmitted to the Young Turks, from them to the Kemalists," [interesting enough,] "the Kemalists were even more decisive than the Young Turks in shaping the state and society with these ideas" (Kuru, 2011:212). "Ziya Gökalp," M. Kemal's chief advisor on sociological issues, "was especially under the influence of Durkheiman Positivism. He also believed that positivism could replace religion" (Demir, 2004:63). The concept of Westernism was developed and spread by Gökalp. According to this view, "the Western civilization must be adopted in order to advance. The Eastern civilization is an obstacle against advancing and the Western civilization is a cause for rising," "Turkism is a direction finder in the phase of establishing a new Turkish state as an ideological movement" (Demir, 2004:77,75).

As a result of westernization being seen as more of political and military necessity, the new leading elite came out especially from among soldiers. As they were trained according to a western value system, this rank was almost totally "estranged from the culture and tradition of [their own] society" (Demir, 2004:54). "The civil aims of the revolutionaries, i.e. the political and social modernization of Turkey ... were not paralleled by popular demands" (Mardin, 1971:199), as the Turkish Revolution was not realized to meet the factual needs of the society it was born in, and was not either "the instrument of a discontented bourgeoisie, it did not ride on a wave of peasant dissatisfaction with the social order, and it did not have as target the sweeping away of feudal privileges, but it did take as a target the values of the Ottoman ancient regime" (Mardin, 1971:202-203). Accordingly, "together with secularism and Westernization, nationalism became one leg of the ideological tripod of young Turkey. Defying the Ottoman past, Atatürk and the ruling Republican People's Party (Cumhuriyet Halk Partisi—CHP) attacked the Ottoman legacy" (Çağaptay, 2006:2). Gradually in the course of time, "'civilization' replaced Islam as the fundamental value of the Turkish Republic, and then 'civilization' became further defined as western civilization ... Atatürk feared the Islamic establishment (in all its forms—the Caliphate, ulama, madrasas, sharia courts, dervishes, etc.) as a focus of his enemies and as a force hostile to his ideals. He therefore set about methodically reducing its influence" (Mango, 1968:228). As a natural outcome of this dominant ideology, *the renunciation of inheritance,* during the first quarter century of the Republic, "the country was laid open to Western cultural and intellectual currents" (Ülman and Tachau, 1965:159). Along this process of *lynching the Ottoman past,* "it was necessary to criticize tradition and especially the ulama and to lose its reliability in the eyes of the public for success" (Demir, 2004:86), "criticizing and discrediting scholars to demonstrate that they cannot represent Islam, to ensure that they [Republicans] are trusted instead of scholars" (Demir, 2004:288). To reach that end, "intellectuals have heavily criticized Islam as it has been implemented throughout history, religious institutions and traditions and especially religious scholars ... in order to ensure that their rhetoric is effective on the public intellectuals tried to undermine the trust of the public towards scholars in the area of religion" (Demir, 2004:372-373). As "the ulama under the leadership of the Shaykh-al-Islam in the Ottoman system or men of religion in a very wide sense played a major role in the central bureaucracy of the government, as well as taking on important responsibilities in local governments all the way from religious services to education, from the interpretation of the law to judicial services, from the managing of foundations to tax collections at certain places" (Kuru, 2011:201), "Kemalist revolutions have caused transformations in political institutions and eliminated the political influence of the ulama" (Kuru, 2011:215). As an unsurprising result, "(Mustafa) Kemal adopted a model that orders the restriction of religion wholly into the private domain and the complete secularization of social life" (Candiotti, quoted by Kuru: 2011:216).

As Bozdoğan and Kasaba argue, "Mustafa Kemal ... saw modernity as both secular and antithetical to parts of Turkey's cultural past. Kemal wanted to "inscribe a firm signature of science and reason" by transforming the individual Turk into a modern rational subject" (1997:26) by attack[ing] "history, using modernizing measures to sever the present from a cultural past" (Aguiar, 2007:106). His formula for modernization "called for immediate, uncompromising westernization and a concomitant rejection of traditional Islamic structures and systems; independent nationalistic props in legend, history, literature, and language were not yet available in sufficient quantity to play a leading role in this transformation" (Perry, 1985:306) because "westernization was not merely a matter of administrative techniques and political institutions; it was fundamentally a transvaluation of values, a transformation of one's view of oneself, of one's history, and of one's place in the body politic" (Kedourie, 1968:21). Under the light of the ideology of westernization, "the Kemalist regime was primarily preoccupied by political and cultural reforms in order to consolidate its newly born revolutionary power and to make Turkey a modern Western country. Education was secularized, Islamic legal codes were replaced by Western codes" (Bayar, 1996:774). The main purpose of the Turkish revolution was obvious enough: "to remove the religious elements from all institutions taken over from the Ottoman Empire that regulate public administration and social life and replace them with worldly and contemporary ones" (Mazıcı, 2011:251).

Clearly motivated by the ideologies of the new Republic, the authorities of the new regime established the Directorate of Sensory Industries and its commission in 1926 and attached it to the National Education Ministry for the purpose of arranging and directing artistic activities. In this way, "taken under the protection of the state, art [was] accepted as one of the foundations required for the survival of the state that is the driving force of the culture policy" (Öndin, 2003:69-70). Çokyiğit points out the role assigned to the artists in those times: "as it is for intellectuals, the fate of artists in our country is to deal with social, political, economic and ethical traumas that occur as a result of westernization from top to bottom ... The intellectual/artist distinction that started in the Ottoman times around Turkic, Islamic, westernist ideas, worked in favor of Turkic and westernist sides in the first years of the Republic (Çokyiğit, 2010:97). Likewise, Nusret Kemal's critique published in 1933 in the journal *Ülkü* concerning Muhsin Ertuğrul's film titled *'Söz Bir Allah Bir' (One Word, One God)* sheds enough light to the issue: For Koçer, Nusret Kemal assigns a mission to Turkish cinema in those times: "Spreading the revolution throughout the nation, becoming instrumental in the establishment and development of national culture in accordance with new admissions, providing the instructive entertainment to the public that develops beautiful tastes, promoting the Turkish nation, the Turkish public and the Turkish revolution abroad" (Koçer, 2010:434). That in/formal mission was being realized parallel to the aims of the reforms of the new Republic as "the Republic was ignoring the past, tradition, culture and art and was attempting to establish its own culture, art, literature, cinema and music. A similar aristocracy that would be created in education, politics, and economy would also be created in art. This was a mandatory period when western understanding and contents were used from literature to poetry, from music to theater and cinema" (Tunç, 2010:167). Along the process of RPP's indoctrination of art education, "the radio, the movie, the opera and the theater were to be used for educational purposes (Howard, 1939:80). Even theaters were ideologized as "after 1932, the government took the initiative in bringing the theatre under fuller control by changing the location, purifying it of immoral, ill-mannered messages, and filling it with its own ideology ... These were government-funded institutions that were to educate the populace, familiarizing them with reforms and new ideology (Öztürk, 2006:303). No surprise, along the years of the new Republic, "the mission of the Turkish University (*Darulfunun*), the Turkological Institute (*Turkiyat Encümeni*), the theater (*Darulbedayi*), and the Conservatory (*Darulelhan*) was the inoculation of the European character to different branches of national culture" (Safarian, 2004:223).

M. Kemal Atatürk's Personal Attitude towards Cinema

For the purpose of "the creation of a modern secular nation with a republican form of government based on the popular will, ... Atatürk defined the principles of his program as Republicanism, Nationalism, Populism, Etatism, Secularism, and Revolutionism (Reformism). These six principles were incorporated into the constitution in 1937. A continuous effort was made to disseminate this ideology" (Szyliowicz, 1966:271-272). However, there was a dramatic problem for the Republicans: the law rate of literacy and the scarcity of the apparatuses of the government to disseminate the ideology. Then the visual aid, cinema, came to the rescue. As Lenin declared a few years before the Turkish Revolution "cinema is the most important art for us [them]" (Nowell-Smith, 2003:386), Atatürk also attached a considerable importance to the art of cinematography since the great majority of both societies were illiterate along the days of revolutions. Likewise, Dorsay points out that Atatürk said "the invention of cinema was more important than the inventions of electricity and continents and it would change the fate of the world" (Dorsay, 1998:3163).

Besides, M. Kemal is reported to have "wanted Russian directors experienced in making propagandistic documentaries to make a movie about his life;" [Interesting enough], "rather than having a professional actor depict him, Atatürk suggested that he [himself] portray himself, that he wear his old clothes and act out what he had done in previous years. Such a movie, however, was never made" (Özyürek, 2004:384). He used to go to movies on all occasions (Özuyar, 2004:69-70). One of the most essential evidences displaying the significance M. Kemal attaches upon cinema is his attitude along the process of filming the movie firstly titled as On the Way to the Victory (Zafer Yollarında), then as Independence (Istiklal) between 1922 and 1942): "He saw the film in 1934 and did not find it good enough and ordered to keep working. After that, a special commission was set up and worked more. Following the whole process and learning that the film had not been completed just because there were not enough moving images in the parts where he himself would appear, he put his reaction into words as "I am alive ... would not I realize my part if you had called me to work in person? I would embrace such an offer, and play my part like an actor and revive my memoirs. This is a national mission" (Saygıner, 1959). For Muhsin Ertuğrul's film *"A Nation is Awakening,"* Atatürk displayed a close interest, "earlier he read and liked the script—especially [went] in front of the camera and repeat[ed] the speech he [would] give at the assembly for the film" (Makal, 2003:76). Atatürk requested Faruk Kenç, another eminent director of that time, to "prepare an extensive report on Turkish cinema," however, "he could not present the report he prepared to Atatürk due to his worsening illness" (Hazar, 2010:186).

Early Days of Cinema of the Republic and Muhsin Ertuğrul, the Dictatorial Director of the Single-Party Period

The themes of the films produced between 1923 and 1940 were almost the same: "the heroism of national war of independence and advocacy of the Republic; the essential tonation of those films were upon modernization preserving the national essence" (Behçetogulları, 2002:107). Along the first years of the Republic, cinema was "the most appropriate tool to be used in the cultural and educational struggle" (Özön, 1995:54). The government must have noticed this fact as they enacted a law on "technical and educational films" in 1937 (Abisel, 1994:47), (Öztürk, 2005:28,155-205). Russian directors were appointed to make a film about the 10th anniversary of the Republic. After the film titled '*Ankara, the Heart of Turkey* (1934)' *(Türkiye'nin Kalbi Ankara (1934)*, "a special production agency, Ha-Ka Film, too, invited a Russian director and made him make a film titled '*Moves of Advancement along the Turkish Revolution*' *(Türk İnkılabında Terakki Hamleleri) (1934-1937)* which dealt with the War of Independence and republican revolutions" (Özön, 1983:1879). The role that rural cinema played was rather significant in social life during the initial years of the Republic as "it has assisted society to adapt to this change, has led the way for the public to request this transformation via the images shown on the screen of the comparison of the old and the new" (Özuyar, 2004:61).

As of Muhsin Ertuğrul, Ali Murat Güven utters less in volume but says much in context: He argues that Ertuğrul was "the 'single director' of the single party period." Güven additionally points out that he was "the first director who took on the task of depopularizing the old. Therefore, it is Muhsin Ertuğrul who invented all the negative clichés used to berate religion, religious men and men of religion in Turkish cinema. Adapting the theater play by Mushipzade Celal, "*Aynaroz Kadısı—Religious Judge of Aynaroz*" to the cinema in 1938, Ertuğrul has thus created the first example of the "bribe-taking, cheating, sex-addicted man of religion that always takes the side of the powerful rather than the just" stereotype in Turkish cinema" (Güven, 2009:3,105-106), (Lüleci, 2009:55). Muhsin Ertuğrul directed 14 films between 1930 and 1939, along which he turned his face totally to the West: *İstanbul Sokaklarında* (1931), *Kaçakçılar* (1929/1932), *Bir Millet Uyanıyor* (1932), *Karım Beni Aldatırsa* (1933), *Söz Bir Allah Bir* (1933), *Cici Berber* (1933), *Fena Yol* (1933), *Mi lyon Avcıları* (1934), *Leblebici Horhor* (1934), *Aysel, Bataklı Damın Kızı* (1934/1935), *Aynaroz Kadısı* (1938), *Bir Kavuk Devrildi* (1939), *Allahın Cenneti* (1939), *Tosun*

Paşa (1939). Almost all of these films were made "under the impact of the French Theatre, German Theatre and commercial cinema, and the Russian revolutionist cinema" (Scognamillo, 2003:42). For Refiğ, one of the eminent milestones of the Turkish Cinema, "this style of cinema by Muhsin, who was the only director during the random westernization efforts of the single party regime, reflected the thinking style and understanding of art of its age very well" (Refiğ, 1971:89). Let us give an ear to the words of Ertuğrul himself that obviously display his philosophy of cinema and film making totally framed by the Western understanding: „if we want to be rehabilitated after all these disasters, we are obligated to accept the principles followed by civilized nations" (Sevinçli, 1987:80). The worse, Ertuğrul displays an open enmity towards the cultural inheritance left by the Ottomans as he once declared "whatever is old and worn out must be demolished, finished: They must be replaced by new ones without using the rubble from the old, let the young ones come" (Sevinçli, 1987:226). The stress was totally upon the Republic and the republican revolutions along his films. Uçakan clarifies the affective perspective upon this notion of Ertuğrul very well:

> The period 1922-39 is covered by Muhsin Ertuğrul on his own. Raised in the west with western culture and famous with being imitative, this man has come to the point of imitating the thoughts and behavior of western people and examples of western cinema frame by frame and took the support of the government behind him to keep Turkish cinema in his monopoly for 17 years. This tendency of his to imitate could be seen as the repetition of political life of the day in the cinema. In all of Ertuğrul's films, the violent purposelessness and desire to westernize of the day can be seen clearly. (Uçakan, 2010:27-28).

M. Ertuğrul's impact on the cinema of the first years of the Republic was so deep and extraordinary that Lüleci declares "it is not a situation often encountered in the cinema of another country for an artist to be influential over the cinema of his own country for such a long time, [in accordance with Ertuğrul's dominance] the films of this era were produced with the thought of coming together around the 'national conscience' and the Republic and that their most important features were the criticism of the old order and the demeaning of the sultanate, khalifdom and religious institutions in order to validate the official state ideology" (Lüleci, 2009:52). "Since Ertuğrul assists in the idea of westernization with his films that are foreign to the realities of Turkish society, he actually carries the identity of the official cinematographer of the Single Party. Along the life styles prescribed in these films, it is obviously witnessed that the formal authority developed the practice of creating a 'unique model of citizen" by means of cinematographic representations (Battal, 2006:109):

> During the period until the 1940's it is obvious that the Turkish cinema was serving the mechanism of creating a deep nationalism with the description of Robins and Aksoy, as a branch of the Kemalist society, where a collective process can be seen operating in the direction of the normalization of cultural homogenization against cultural diversity ... As a result of the project of designing a Kemalist nation, it equips the identity of the new Turk with a modernist consciousness completely independent from the Ottomans, in the sense of politics and culture, where Islamic references are removed, where different ethnic identities are created and oppressed. (Maktav, 2010:43).

A clear attack on religious values and figures during the Republican period was observed along the films Ertuğrul made: "Films made during 1938-1939 such as *Aynaroz Kadısı (The Moslem Judge of Aynaroz), Bir Kavuk Devrildi (A Turban was Toppled)* by Muhsin Ertuğrul, men of religion and hodjas were mocked in both films adapted from plays of Musahipzade Celal" (Özgüç, 2005:187). As a result of films of Muhsin Ertuğrul assaulting spiritual values of the public, "the pious public has cooled off from cinema [and] saw as a sin even film watching ... [since] religious characters were presented in the Turkish cinema as liars, cheaters, sex offenders and traitors; [and] this negative attitude started with the single director of the single party period, Muhsin Ertuğrul" (Enderun, 2011:10,12). For instance, the film *A Nation is Awakening* produced by Ertuğrul in 1932 takes on our National Struggle. The main character of this film, 'Molla Said' is depicted as a traitorous man of religion collaborating with the invasion forces. In the film *If My Wife Cheats On Me* he produced in 1933, he "displays Turkish girls in bathing suits for the first time ... in another film made by Muhsin Ertuğrul in 1933, *One Word, One God,* the figures are modern characters; in terms of their appearances, the places they live in, etc. they represent the targeted Western face of the new Turkey but the man-woman relationships among them are excessively 'liberal' relationships even for the most modern sections of the Turkey of the 30's. The relations occurring between the rowing instructor and women at a marine sports classroom, men who lust after their friends' wives or girlfriends, or woman characters who cheat on their husbands or fiancés, revue girls dancing wearing scanty outfits" (Lüleci, 2009:54).

Considering the parallelism and conformity between Ertuğrul's production philosophy and the ideological aims of the new Republic, it does not become hard to deduce that Ertuğrul connived with the actors of the new Turkish Republic and revolutions. Though it might not be considered as the single factor, we are not to ignore that "Ertuğrul and his cast—who mostly stayed unchanged—were waged by the government as they were the staff members of the Istanbul Municipal Theatre" (Büker, 2002:153). The fact that "there is a great conformance between the policy of the era and the messages the films are trying to convey, put forth as an ideological polemic" (Lüleci, 2009:52) (Menekşe, 2005:46), does not turn out to be a great surprise "despite the lack of [an open] government contribution to the cinema the ruling directors of the times have made films in conformance with the effective values of the Republic for a long time" (Kayalı, 2006:23). During this period the official ideology is aware of the role of cinema in social transformation but has not made a decision about which method to follow in providing this transformation. Visualization in cinema of certain values underlined from the point of view of the nation state brings out natural doubts that there was a vague conspiration, albeit not obvious officially, between the Turkish cinema sector and the government. Values adapted through films of traditional Turkish cinema conform to the policies in force in the Turkey of the period in a restructuring process. At this time it can be said that there was a conforming structure between the cinema and the state. Although the government was not too close to the cinema sector and did not provide it material support, the narration of the melodramas and the values offered conform to the political discourse. In the same vein, indicating that there are similarities between the traditional Turkish Cinema and the historical development process of the new Republic, Dorsay declares:

> Truly, the history of the Republican period and the history of our cinema carry an unbelievable level of similarities and points of intersection. During the 'national chief' period started with Atatürk founding the Republic and putting into motion the revolutions, there is only one single name in cinema, a national cinematographer: Muhsin Ertuğrul. Just as the lack of staff, the lack of the adequate personnel in every area during the Atatürk period reinforced the 'one man' feature of this period (perhaps a little despite Atatürk himself) there is no staff or cinematographer in cinema. (Dorsay, 2003:45).

Public Houses and Village Chambers

Public houses and village chambers were established to transport and disseminate Kemalist nationalism discourses to the society (Yeğen, 1999:44,173), (Szyliowicz, 1966:270), (Özön, 1995:55). The Public Houses were established on February 19th, 1932. The aim of their establishment was "the application of the culture policy base their activities on two missions; having social reforms adapted and conducting cultural and artistic events to provide for contemporization" (Öndin, 2003:80,84) (Karaömerlioğlu, 1998:68). Public Houses were definitely controlled by the People's Party (the only party allowed to exist) and naturally serve as channels for national propaganda. Karpat argues "their purpose was to bridge the gap between the intelligentsia and people by teaching the first of these the national culture which lay among the Anatolian masses and, the second, the rudiments of civilization, and an indoctrination of the nationalist secular ideas of the Republican regime" (1963:55). The Public Houses were "designed to serve as agencies for political communication and socialization. . .The constant emphasis was upon modernization, laicism, and nationalism, and they served to create a favorable climate for the values of the modernizing elite" (Szyliowicz, 1966:272). Films that were surely sent or bought by RPP, government or Public Houses were run free to the public as the films were considered to be modern "tools of indoctrination" (RPP Public Houses Manual, 1935, article 69). In accordance with this notion, "7850 films were run between 1932 and 1940 in the Public Houses all over the country" (Kılınç, 2005:164). In 1938, "there were more than two hundred of these People's houses offering conferences, lectures, concerts, moving pictures, drama, etc., to the people" (Howard, 1939:82).

1950-1960: Multi-Party System and Coup D'état

As Oktay argues 1950s are mostly known to be the years when the single party totalitarism ended and the commerce and industry bourgeois rose up to sovereignty (2002:87). Along the government period of DP (Democrat Party), "a type of activism that did not have a distinct system and open objectives turned into state policy. A rough experientialism replaced the intellectual and cultural concerns that ruled during 1923-46. No matter what the source may be, "economic power became the basic criterion that determines social position" (Karpat, 2011:199). "The traditional conservative ideology had changed" after 50ies (Belge, 1983:846). After transforming into multi-party system, the society was totally "surrounded by the ideology of consumerism," and the traditional culture "had been substantially visualized" (Oktay, 1987:50). There happened an ideological revolution caused by the economic transformation framed only after that the DP came to power. The change was not a minor one: "earlier social values, based on education and dedication to state ideals, were undermined by an order based essentially on economic power. Socially and psychologically this was a far-reaching revolution. Materially and morally, it affected every single section of the traditional ruling groups; the civil bureaucracy, the military, and all their affiliates" (Karpat, 1966:178).

Regarding the impact of DP era on the art of cinematography Şen argues that "the coming to power of the Democratic Party in 1950 meant that Anatolia would be visible throughout the country as much as the idea of change. The translation of this into the cinema would be the reflection of the stories of Anatolian people to the silver screen rather than stories adapted from foreign sources or those who take a certain sect as an audience" (Şen, 2010:17). In this sphere of liberal cosmopolitanism, the field of cinema was filled up with many names that were so far to the artistic creativity or aesthetics of the art. The situation was so abnormal and negative that the eminent directors of the era had not backgrounds related directly to cinema. This would not be regarded as a trifle detail since "throughout the 1950's critics, the cinema lodge and intellectuals have not come to terms for the artistic, economic and cultural development of Turkish Cinema" (Yıldırım, 2010:33). For example, "Akad had studied art history education, Metin Erksan wrote cinema articles in newspapers and journals, and he was followed by Atıf Yılmaz who was interested in paintings after studying art and Memduh Ün who played for the Besiktas football team and entered cinema first as a player then a producer" (Şen, 2010:17). To have a close view on the impacts of Turkey's socio-economic-cultural structure on cinema between the years of 1950-1975 shall shed a light to the argument: one of the most influential events of this era is the 1948 tax reduction. Municipal tax that was taken from cinema incomes was reduced with a law passed in 1 July 1948. Entertainment tax taken from cinemas by municipalities was determined as 25% of revenue in the cinemas which run Turkish film and 70% in which run foreign film. Reducing tax rate provides the waking of cinema industry; cinemas preferred to run Turkish films. People had preferred Turkish films to foreign films especially in Anatolia. In this case, inclination towards native characters has started in cinema. Because, Turkish society wanted to watch its own culture, traditions and own people in cinema. The era of emulation to American life style and consumption has started as a result of this policy. Migrations to overseas and from the rural regions to the urban have begun. Istanbul has become the most migration-receiving city. People who migrated from rural to urban and started living in slums have brought their own culture and life styles together. Slum culture and arabesque culture have been formed spontaneously.

50s witnessed the starting days of domestic migration in Turkey, from rural areas to the cities since "the rule of splitting the land among siblings coming from inheritance law caused the land of the small land owners to become even smaller. The inability of this shrinking land to feed the family has necessitated migration to the city. The spreading of the land highways throughout the whole country, the economic system creating a consumer society, the livening of trade and non-agriculture activities were factors that facilitated the decision to migrate from the rural areas to the city" (Esen, 2000:102). In another short time interval these migrants often must evolve their own social norms and cultural patterns in order to adapt successfully to their new milieu. Along with the arrival of an individual to leave behind his village and primary relationships to the city, a new urbanization process started for Turkish society. With its own unique constitution, this process involved some conflicts for the individual while becoming accustomed to urban living; it also transported values and manners belonging to rural like to the city. This is highlighted as the most important aspect preparing the creation of village-cities, which are a part of formative modernization. Sencer points out another dimension of migration as he argues "migration to big cities has increased to a great extent in this era ... In the migration process, experiencing differentness has seen in the flow of society to the big cities. Considering accordingly, an urbanization process has been experienced based on migrations that were originated from surplus rural population before 1950, unemployed [people] and agricultural laborers between 1950-1960, those who left agricultural occupations as for the era between 1960-1970" (Sencer, 1979:168).

On the side of politics, the migration played a dramatic role as well. As Ahmad notes "the peasantry never benefited from the secular culture created by the Kemalist state. That did not matter until the multi-party period when its vote began to count and when peasants became consumers in a growing capitalist society. As they became more confident of their rights as citizens, they began to make demands on the political parties and the state, demands which could not be easily disregarded. Gaining the vast majority, the peasants began to transform the political and cultural landscape of the secular Turkey" (Ahmad, 1988:758). Along the period, "many works consisting of stories and novels "with social content" written after 1950, reflected trends of thought constituting a foundation to a new leftism. Mahmut Makal, Yasar Kemal, Orhan Kemal, Aziz Nesin, Kemal Tahir, Fakir Baykurt, Kemal Bilbasar, Atilla Ilhan and Necati Cumali. They wanted to tell their readers about the unknown dimensions of the social problems experienced in Turkey, poverty, frustrations and injustice" (Karpat, 2011:85). On the part of the conservatives, cinema gained an opportunity to represent history in a liberalized way: "the fact that the Ottomans were not all bad and that they at least had some bright pages being reflected into the cinema did not take place until 1950. It is not a coincidence that this date overlapped the time of multi-parties in politics" (Dumanlı, 2009:99).

1960-12 September 1980: An Era of Polarization and Confusion

In 1960, Turkish democratic life took a major blow, the military junta took the power, judged the elected president and two ministers of his cabinet in front of an antidemocratic military court and hanged them charging with flimsy crimes. Leftist people called this coup as a revolution whereas no one still knows what actually revoluted was. Karpat argues the coup "removed social structures lingering from the old order albeit unwittingly. Constitutionalism, parliamentarism and liberalism, that are the traditional values of the middle class, became the most basic political belief in the new order. The majority of the Assembly was made up of CHP members or their proponents" (Karpat, 2011:154). General Gürsel, the head of the junta, "openly declared that socialism might be beneficial to Turkey" (Karpat, 1966:181), and, "Turkey need[ed] social reforms and that socialism should [have] be[en] seen as a proper vehicle for development made the social targets of the revolution quite apparent" (Karpat, 2011:152), "including President Cemal Gürsel, leading members of the military government did not refrain from openly stating that socialism could be useful for Turkey" (Karpat, 2011: 88). From the perspective of today, it is clearly deduced that along the 1960s political debates, there developed a split on the social structure of the country: conservatives emphasizing on the particularities of Turkey, on its internal dynamics thereby focusing on issues of identity, or culture in general and a subsequent will to derive of the social from the cultural, and, the modernists insisting on social progress, economic development and the subsequent derivation of the cultural from the social. In tune with these frameworks, modernists sided with universal values, equalized generally with western culture, as the more universally taken the sphere of the cultural be related to further progress, whereas nationalists or traditionalists in general worked with a more determinate set of values unique to the nation's, or the community's context, as the search for identity would necessitate such a delimited cultural understanding.

Then, the 1961 Constitution came on the stage which had been totally framed by the military junta and their abettors from media, judiciary and academy who mostly were sheer socialists or indirect advocators of socialist system. As Karpat notes, "the founding assembly preparing the Constitution was in control of CHP and some socialists (Karpat, 2011:88). The noteworthy aspect of the 1961 Constitution was that it seemed to have guaranteed the freedom of science and art. According to its 21st article, "everyone has the right of learning, teaching, explaining, spreading science and art freely and making all kinds of searching in these fields" (Soysal, 1997:68). In other words, "the Constitution adopted after the 27 May 1960 Coup brought freedom to westernist idea, art and culture movements of every color and shade ... Westernist left intellectuals cared greatly for cinema naturally as they did for all western arts" (Çokyiğit, 2010:98). The junta had the supporters of the coup made a few films in 1960 and 1961 that were totally serving to revile the democratically elected people. The mere titles of the films were enough to understand what the films were about: *Rascals in Yassıada (1960), The Lawdown of Rascals (1961)*. The films were run all over the country to propagate the ideology of the coup and to vindicate the military intervention. After the confounded coup of 1960, new scapegoats were created in Turkish society and these were shown as those guilty of Turkey's social and economic backwardness. Newspaper correspondents got busy trying to find villages that were in the ownership of radical landlords in the rural area. Through the means of mass media, it was announced that the landlords and their collaborators, religious leaders, would make sure that villagers would remain ignorant and they could continue to exploit them. Some imaginary capitalists were accused of not paying the workers the wages they deserved. Countless evidences were fabricated 'proving' that wealth was collected in the hands of certain people in an unjust manner during the DP rule. Then, It was offered that this sick situation would be remedied by a regime ran by the elite possessing social consciousness. On the other hand, 27 May coup "became the liberation of left thought in 1960s," political and ideological structure of the era directly revealed itself along the development that took place in the Turkish Cinema of that time (Altuğ, 1973:55). After the coup, "discussion of ideological concepts had started. Films that contain ideological themes or that are related to sociological events also appeared during this period" (Maraşlı, 2010:108) until the year of 1965, when JP (Justice Party) took the power (Coş, 1987:52).

One of the most significant phenomena of the era was the domestic migration, from rural area to the cities. For those migrated poor masses in 60es, "cinema was the only and cheapest pass time activity. As a result of this, film production rose in an overwhelming speed: "As only 68 films had been made in 1960, 229 films were made in 1966" (Özön, 1985:368); "the photographed news stories of the tabloid press concerning film stars" (Esen, 2000:32) was another eminent element. Arslan related the situation of the Turkish cinema of 60s to "the feeling of [the] dream and the impossibility of creating a closed identity, with the extension of the destructive energy of modernity and capitalism, that it is divided between the promise of autonomy of the Turkish Cinema and trapped by an uneasy melancholy into moral conversion by this tragic language" (2010:248). The most productive fruit of this antidemocratic era, perhaps, became that varying ideas rooted by different ideologies came up about what should cinema be/come in Turkey. The eminent cinematographers of that period gathered around varying philosophical cinema approaches, such as National Cinema, Revolutionist Cinema, etc., and tried to make films conforming to their ideological and philosophical stances.

The *Yeşilçam* Legend: More than a Street of Film and Cinema

The films are called as *Yeşilçam* films that left a mark on Turkish Cinema history and were shot between 1950s and 70s. *Yeşilçam* actually was the name of the street where most of the offices of the directors and the cafes the actors and actresses used to gather around. Interesting enough, the rise of *Yeşilçam* was too much depended upon the policies of the political parties. Rising films in the era of DP pumped a liberal capitalist ideology to the society that was somewhat framed by that the primary goal of life was dolce-vita, an epicurean, hedonist life style. Abisel notes that "the concept of *Yeşilçam* has appeared by changing of the production relations in Turkish Cinema and increasing of the production companies. This period not easily, can be made definite as 1960-1975" (1997:123). The films were composed of popular fictions which enabled masses to spend their leisure time either amusing or crying. Along this period, an increase in the amount of films and film houses was observed that of course made a great support to the construction of Turkish cinema as an industry or commercial institution, though unfortunately this process has not yet been completed. Whereas a success and advancement might be mentioned regarding to the quantitative value, the same could not be asserted in terms of qualitative features.

1950s onwards, specific distribution methods—such as percentage distribution and delayed-discounted distribution—are merged with the traditional method in which the same film would be re-released in different times, and led to a production type unique to the Turkish Cinema Industry. A unique production-financing method called as "region industry" initiated the development of Turkish cinema along that era. The problem was that this system caused the decrease of production quality in the long term. The system operated in a simple way: there were region managers. They would give reports to the producers about which type of films were in demand, tell what kind of film (determining topics, actors and actresses, even directors) they wanted and producers would shape almost all features of the films they would make according to the demands of the region managers—indirectly to the audience's. In proportion to the extent of the advance taken from these in return for the further income of the film, authorities of these on the choice of topic, script and actor/actress increase. In other words, producers were totally and directly dependent on the public demand. This feed-back based production system accelerated the rise of "star system" as the Turkish Cinema did not have a liberal economic infrastructure like in the contemporary cinemas in the same era. But regarding the psycho-sociological concerns, these films were able to take people away from their daily problems and would allow them to live in a fairytale environment and experience happy endings, which has ever been the basic wish of all the governments all along the history of humanity. Uçakan describes those years as follows:

> Decreases in the municipal taxes up to 70%, electrifying of the rural centers and the boom in the film houses transform the production of cinema to a gold mine. A flow starts to Yeşilçam in 1950s and small merchants from the every side of the country run to Istanbul for film-making. There is not an enough infrastructure supporting this rapid numerical increase: "The most interesting aspect of this event is that almost all of the comers to Yeşilçam are people who come out of the community themselves. Those people who are far from the intellectual sensibility would not have concerns about art, ideology of course. (Uçakan, 2010:20).

Arslan quotes Ayşe Şasa commenting on the phenomenon of *Yeşilçam* in a way much is displayed: "it can comfortably be said that Yeşilcam cinema has its peculiar folkloric and popular poeticism that is village-like, Lumpen and complex free with Şasa having its own poetry in the ummah period ... Şasa searches for our own cinematography in the clues of neighborhood cinema. He makes a call for abandoning a stillborn imitative cinema technique and looking at it through a point of view that is specific to our own culture" (Arslan, 2010:269). For Akerson, things never look as they are since "Turkish Cinema was not born as the fruit of an industrial revolution as it happened in the West. It is however the production of the certain economics of consumption that were created by the western production styles in the developing countries. 1948, the foundation year of Turkish Cinema, indicates at the same time the process of existence of a new social class that developed through the economics of consumption" (quoted by Daldal, 2005:35). Uçakan points out the same economical factor where he declares that "they [the film producers of 1950-75] only had two purposes. Let's have fun and earn money. Through this slogan ... they pushed cinema to the remotest corners of Turkey. They brought the preference of the people from the periphery to the center with their observations and intuition" (2010:30).

'Easy money and entertainment' was the essential philosophy embedded throughout the films produced along this era that was closely parallel to the political slogans echoing in the streets. For Nezih Erdoğan, some other complications too were involved: "modernity or the western life style were presented something that must have definitely been reached but needed at the same time the healing and even saving intervention of the lower classes and Anatolian values against the peril of corruption" (2001:5). Among many other similar interpretations, Refiğ attracts attentions with his quite positive approach towards Yeşilçam as he declares that "starting in the initial years of the coming to power of the Democratic Party, the Yeşilcam cinema is a forward and positive step in the history of our cinema as it has features of the opening of cinema to the public just like the opening of politics to the people in the same years" (Refiğ, 1971:89). The surprising advancement in *Yeşilçam* could not be conceived without taking "the new audience" into consideration. Ayça described this new audience as "the people of closed society structure, the traditional rural oral culture;" they were "conservative and traditionalist in culture and met the cinema first time in their lives. And Yeşilçam was a cinema produced for this audience" (2003:23) (Daldal, 2003:43–44). In accordance with the expectations of this "new audience," *Yeşilçam* films produced love stories with happy endings that represented the conservative and traditional ideology which regards the family and honor as the top values; legitimizes the inequality of genders and violence against females. Indicating the link between the production mentality of *Yeşilçam* and the social demand, Refiğ argues that "Turkish cinema is not the cinema of imperialism since it was not established by foreign capital, is not bourgeois cinema since it was not established by national capitalism, is not state cinema since it was not established by the government ... Turkish cinema is a "public cinema" since it originated from the need of the Turkish public and is based on labor, not capital" (1971:80). Due to this fact of being public, people used to go to movies as families, which caused many people called this era as 'the golden age of Turkish cinema'. Of course, the fact that those films presented a section of the lives of that 'new audience', their living environment, and people in their neighborhood, characters and types in a tale format played a crucial role. Accordingly, the distinctive economic structure of Turkish cinema has led the scriptwriters and directors of those times to contact with society and understand audience's emotional situation, as well.

National (Milli) Cinema[1]: The Conservative Emphasis on Theological and Ethical Values

Hazar defines Milli cinema as "an ecole created by some youngsters who wished to serve their ideas by ideological methods" (2004), while Yenen claims that Milli Cinema trend expressed "the realizations of limited religious representations in Turkish Cinema through the thought of Islamism. And because of this, it displayed a progress parallel to the chronological course of Turkish Islamism. The eminent directors

---

1 Yaylagül endeavours to clarify the huge difference between the maps of meaning of two so-called synonym words, 'milli' and 'ulusal': "The concepts of 'Ulusal' and 'Milli' represent two different trends in Turkish cinema. Thus, although as far as literal meaning ulusal and milli are synonymous various segments apply different meanings to these two words. Those using Ulusal claim that Ulusal Cinema is the cinema of Turkish society, whereas those who defend the view of the milli cinema claim that the real national cinema is the cinema of the Turkish nation, the milli cinema. Although both segments are using two synonymous words, the meanings that these concepts denote for the parties are as different as mountains" (2004:268). However, this effort is not enough. The story of these two words dates back to the process of so-called purification of the Turkish Language that took place under the reign of RPP in 40s. The word 'ulusal' was fabricated to replace the Arabic-rooted word 'milli', both meaning 'national' in English. After that, those who have been defining themselves as 'secular' consciously used the word 'ulusal' whereas those defining themselves 'anti-secular, religious or conservative' preferred to use the word 'milli' to mean the same. In other words, two words have become two symbols of two opposite life styles. Regardingly, 'milli cinema' is referred to a much more conservative and religious stance whereas 'ulusal cinema' is mostly related to a secularized nationalism.

of the trend are Yücel Çakmaklı, Mesut Uçakan, İsmail Güneş, Mehmet Tanrısever, Metin Çamurcu, Salih Diriklik, and Nurettin Özel. Three periods are to mention: Milli Sinema: Early Years and The Classical Era (1970–1989), Islamic Cinema: The Peak Era (1989–1995), Conservative Cinema: The Era of Recession (1995–2010)" (Yenen, 2012:240-244). Maraşlı argues that Çakmaklı considered that "national cinema should be a school, and created the Cinema Club at the MTTB (National Unity of Turkish Students)[2] that was organizing cinema shows, discussion meetings, forums, seminars and other meetings under this roof. Thus, the national cinema movement started to gain momentum. University youth who were interested in cinema would gather around the club and continue their education. Among these youngsters Dr. Salih Diriklik and Mesut Uçakan were names that stood out. Subsequently, Osman Sınav, İsmail Güneş, Metin Camurcu, Nazif Tunç, Cem Ertürk and Mehmet Tanrısever continued as followers of this movement" (2010:114). For Dorsay, a cinema master in Turkey, Milli Cinema was "one of the most significant cinema trends about the end of 60s and the beginning of 70s which defended the view that many of our problems originated from that we had opened our doors to the West and the culture and values coming from the West, and from our fancy for westernization. Of course it attached great importance to the religion and Islamic principles and considered them as one of the chief pillars of the society" (Dorsay, 1989:112-113). Çakmaklı's stress was upon refreshing the memory of society to purify the corruption caused by the fancy of westernization. This cinema trend offered the prioritization of religious values the single alternative that could evoke the necessary spirit to return to the bright life of the Ottoman Empire.

Regarding the audience side, Yücel Çakmaklı was a director esteemed greatly by the Islamic segment [since] in all the films he made

---

[2] "From its foundation (1916) to the abolition in 1980, MTTB played significant roles on the participation of the university youth in the political life ... MTTB believed that Marxist point of view could not offer solutions to the problems of Turkey as a method in cinema. It assrted that the Marxist methodology shall always stay foreign to understand and analyse the Turkish social structure as much as other western methods" (Maktav, 2004:990), (Anonymous, 1973:18).

during 1970-74 he included themes with religious content. In the forums he attended and in his articles he was a theoretician and proponent of Milli Cinema. Özgüç calls the films made by Milli Cinema ecole simply 'Islamic films' and determines the milestone year of those films as 1970, whereas "Çakmaklı had refused to use the term Islamic cinema" (Maraşlı, 2010:113). Dönmez also claims that "*Milli Sinema* was in fact Islamist cinema, but it could not openly be advertised as such as item 163 of the constitution forbade using religion for such purposes" (Dönmez-Colin, 2004:87). For Özgüç those films "attract[ed] the Turkish people inside Islamic values excluding religious exploitation. This is a 'milli cinema' that seeks its essence in itself, in Islam rather than the West. The creator of this conceptual trend in cinema was Yücel Çakmaklı. *Oğlum Osman (My Son Osman), Kızım Ayşe (My Daughter Ayşe), Memleketim (My Land)* are the first products of the national cinema concept that lasted until 1974. Along the lines of this thought, Çakmaklı portrays the transformation stories of Moslem youth who get confused when facing the Western culture and then returning to its essence and achieving peace" (Özgüç, 2005:189). In respect to this perspective, Milli Cinema appeared as an expression of an understanding that prioritized moral and local values against social estrangement and disintegration based on imitation of the Western cultural values since the local values in new urban lives shaped by the migration from the village to the city especially after the 1970's triggered a factual corruption of the Turkish society. Yücel Çakmaklı's film he made in 1970, *Birleşen Yollar (Roads to Reunite)* is mostly considered to be the first example of Milli Cinema. Çakmaklı's other films in this trend are *Oğlum Osman (My Son Osman), Kızım Ayşe (My Daughter Ayşe)*. The most important point stressed in Çakmaklı's films is that young people, who are estranged from themselves and their essential values, will find the right path only by embracing Islamic values (Çokyiğit, 2010:99).

"Films containing powerful religious messages are started to be seen in the 1970's when the migration from the villages to cities speeded up" (Özdemir, 2011:8) as the new audience was eager to see their values be presented in the cinema. Besides, "there has been a reaction against foreign cinema ever since the first years when national cinema came out. This is an understanding of the cinema whose roots are based on national origins, on our national assets, preservation of our national assets, and the spirit of our national unity. This understanding is especially against internationalism. It is national thought against internationalism" (Maraşlı, 2010:117). Dorsay projects the psychological aspect of Çakmaklı's films noting that "Yücel Çakmaklı struggled to get wide masses to make peace with their belief thoughts ... His topics revolve around the theme of the individual having a belief problem in a modern society." In this way, Dorsay relates Çakmaklı "to directors such as Dreyer, Rossellini, Bergman" (Dorsay, 1989:489). In the same vein, Yücel Çakmaklı himself is quoted clarifying Milli Cinema and its mission related with psycho-sociological perspectives: "we did not tell tales in our films; we tried to show how our Turkish people who have established great civilizations in the past, were pillaged by indiscreet foreign culture agents with their culture and art, how the western culture was tried to be worn to our society like a straitjacket with an invasionist attitude, rather than a humane synthesis" (Özdemir, 2011:10). The same essential aspects of the ecole is consolidated by Gökmen as that "Yücel Çakmaklı places scientific thought, art and religion as bases of Milli Cinema;" and his themes and topics would be taken from Seljukian and Ottoman life styles;" in other words, "the essential values gained throughout the historical process along those ideal periods of Turkish history would be found out and reflected on the cinema" (Gökmen, 1973a:32).

National (*Ulusal*) Cinema: A Quest to Overcome Ages-Long Identity Crisis

The phenomenon of '*Ulusal* Cinema' started circling in the years of 1967-1968, essentially termed and framed by Halit Refiğ, one of the legendary directors of Turkish Cinema. National Cinema prescribed a kind of cinema understanding based upon the approach that every society should be assessed within the framework of their own characteristics and local values, and defended a cinematographic view that is both conforming to the traditional values of society and does not break off realities of the contemporary life. For Diriklik the ecole basically adopted a materialistic approach, no matter it included some references to nationalism: "towards the middle of the 1960's some Marxist authors such as Kemal Tahir, Selahattin Hilac, Sencer Divitcioğlu and their followers some socialist cinematographers who were their followers such as Atıf Yılmaz, Halit Refiğ, Metin Erksan started to develop a new thesis, claiming that the cosmopolitan understanding of culture and art in the Republican period went bankrupt and that we need to go to a materialistic structure within ourselves by rejecting the West" (Diriklik, 1995:16). The 27 May coup had a direct impact on the birth of the ecole since "according to Halit Refiğ the 27 May movement that is a westernization movement in our society was a failure ... While working on Turkish cinema, Refiğ tried to understand the historical origins of the culture of Turkish society and roots of the culture like a sociologist who imprisoned himself within the confines of cinema. This forced Halit Refiğ and the other directors to develop a new theoretical approach to cinema" (Yaylagül, 2004:259). Ulusal cinema directors of National Cinema reactively accused the intellectuals of 60s who desired to embrace Western or universal values in the form and the content of their works, of being western admirers and of being the producers of the ideology of individualism (Yaylagül, 2004:263). Ulusal Cinema was established against to the cosmopolitan profit-motive cinema and the foreign cinemas. Ulusal Cinema was supported neither by the public nor the government. Politics of Justice Party towards to the rather non-liberal Turkish cinema led the directors such as Refiğ, Erksan, and Sağıroğlu towards to the conceptualization of Ulusal Cinema. They conceived a cinema purified from the Marxist point of view. In the leadership of Halit Refiğ, directors such as Metin Erksan and Duygu Sağıroğlu made newly-coded cinema films in order to understand the people and to make films conforming to the cultural texture of the people. Especially, the heavy impact of Kemal Tahir on Halit Refiğ created the mental foundations of these new creations. Refiğ declares the essential points of the ecole as follows:

> In the area of land ownership, the historical evolution of the Ottoman-Turkish society based on the state feudalism and the western societies based on the feudal private ownership took place over sepa-

> rate paths, contrary to Western Europe, a bourgeois class based on the capital of trade and industry did not come about in the Turkish society. The individualistic world view of Western European arts is a feature specific to the bourgeois class. The Turkish public has a collective world view, whose origin is based on migrant Turkish traditions, Islamic law and the Ottoman government system ... The newly raised administrative cast has become a colonial gendarme of western thought and art in its own country knowingly or unknowingly, has constantly removed itself from its public, has started to look at the public in a demeaning manner or even as an enemy. *The attitudes of the Turkish intellectuals who became the colonial gendarmes of the west in thought and art, against Turkish cinema is a result of this* ... It is a scientific fact that the economic and social make-up of the Turkish society is different from western societies accepted today by everyone except for dogmatic Marxists. Therefore, societies with different infrastructures must also have different superstructures. Just as the 'Tımar' system is not the same thing as the feudal system in the west, just as the Ottoman 'sipahis' cannot be compared to the European barons, Turkish spectator arts cannot be likened to the theater of the west. Theater is a product of the social structure of the west. It is an art form that has been attempted to be imposed always from the top to the bottom as a part of the westernization movement ever since the time when the government initiated westernization movements in the Turkish society that does not possess the same social structure, but still has not been accepted by the public as of the present time. (1971:52,73,95).

Before conceptualization of Ulusal Cinema ecole, Refiğ would call the Turkish Cinema as the people's cinema: "Turkish cinema is not the cinema of imperialism since it was not founded by foreign capital and not state cinema since it was not founded by the government. Turkish cinema is the 'people's cinema' since it was originated due to the need of the Turkish public to watch films and since it is based on labor rather than capital" (Refiğ, 1971:87). Not after a long course of time, varying from describing the traditional Turkish cinema as 'people's cinema', Refiğ put forward the concept of Ulusal Cinema in order to underline the reality he observed in society and made films in this direction. Thus, Ulusal Cinema ecole claims to be a cinema of awareness, information provision, a cinema of consciousness concerning the state it is in without being against the basic values of the public. Though Daldal claims that the rise of Ulusal Cinema owes to that Justice Party took the power in 1965 which retarded the socio-realistic cinema view (Daldal, 2005:125), Arslan brings a much more complex initiative to the essence of the ecole noting that "Halit Refiğ ... searches for ways to defend the closed Turkish economy, Turkish art, Turkish thought against the foreign influence of the west and to find its own richnesses that must be returned to. Unsuccessful westernization attempts, the singing of foreign ballads must be left aside; the salvation must be sought in the return to the unspoiled people" (2010:260).

As Tunç praises Refiğ's effort declaring that "Halit Refiğ ... considered feeding the production entirely with domestic resources to be the measure of being national" (2010:169), Kahraman points out that Refiğ's "biggest mistake was that he always organized his thoughts in a government centric manner" (2010:499). For Daldal, on the other hand, Refiğ had been just a member of the socio-realistic view of cinema and changed totally after the year of 1965, when the political power was taken by a rightist party, JP: "Refiğ's love and hate relationship he went through with the west and the relatively 'pragmatic' attitude he took on against this political conjuncture changing after 1965 and his own understanding of socialism that contains some ideological inconsistencies lies in the foundation of this theoretical confusion. But still, until 1965 Refiğ was the most dynamic member of the 'social realist' trend, while making contributions with many important films to this process of Turkish cinema to create an identity" (2005:103). Either this or that way, it could be asserted that 'Ulusal Cinema' trend or ecole made attempts to read the reality of the dramas hidden in the details of the Turkish social structure and tried to realize this specific reading as much as market conditions and political sphere allowed. The process of the creation of Ulusal Cinema can be assessed as an effort to find out a solution to the ages-old identity crisis since the framework of conceptualizations turn around ages-old terms such as the West, Turkish beliefs and traditions, etc. Refiğ made attempts to produce a specific kind of visual art element that the public would like consume, by taking the wishes and background of the public into consideration in order to develop a cinematographic structure that somehow would conform to the Turkish psycho-sociological structure. Uçakan classifies the films that carry the trances of the 'Ulusal Cinema' concept as follows: Bir Türke Gönül Verdim—I Loved a Turk (Refiğ, 1967), Kuyu—Well (Erksan, 1968), Sevmek Zamanı—Time to Love (Erksan, 1965), Fatma Bacı—Sister Fatma (Refiğ, 1972), Vurun Kahbeye—Strike the Harlot (Refiğ, 1973), Hudutların Kanunu—The Law of the Border (Akad, 1966), Ah Güzel Istanbul—Beautiful Istanbul (Batıbeki, 1966), Çalıkusu—Bird in the Bush (Seden, 1966), Kızılırmak-Karakoyun—Red River-Black Sheep (Akad, 1967), Ana—Mother (Akad, 1967), Sinekli Bakkal—Grocer Full of Flies (Dinler, 1967), Yaprak Dökümü—Falling Leaves (Ün, 1967), Zilli Nazife—Nazife's Bells (Ün, 1967), Cemo (Batıbeki, 1975), Kuma—Concubine (Batıbeki, 1975) (Uçakan, 2010:53).

The Cinema of Turkish-Style Social Realism: On the Borderline of a Socialist Simulacrum and Communist Utopia

On 27 May 1960, the Turkish Armed Forces intervened the democratic life in Turkey. Embarrassing enough, they took "the support of the civilians, intellectuals, bureaucrats and the middle class that has entered a state of economic and political crisis as a result of the policies of the DP (Democratic Party) to start a [totalitarian] era in the social life of Turkey ... The fundamental philosophy of the 1961 Constitution also affected the Turkish films made in this period ... Turkish cinema ... started to show interest in social problems" (Yaylagül, 2004:244), mostly in front a communist-revolutionist perspective. The modernization process during the post 1960 era that the society was involved in and the conflicts and controversies around it were a major source for socio-realist films. Irregular urbanization, migration, social and public crises created among city and village dwellers and the impact of modernization over traditional life and the conflicts it creates were considered on the basis of social problems. In this or that way, their discourse dwelled around the assumption that a communist revolution was 'the only way out'.

Along the films of this trend according to Uçakan, "many have taken on the people of the village rather than the proletariat, spiritual values more than material realities, the religious beliefs of the Turkish people, their habits and traditions, while some mocked these, others praised them, therefore moved away from a materialistic attitude, the texture of the events did not reach class analysis. Some of them turned to a nationalism mixed with Marxism by highlighting the bitter results of westernization, while some others made films that turned to realities of the country with good intentions but have no relation to the ideological situation" (Uçakan, 2010:27). Directors of this trend tried to dwell upon the reality of society as far as labor and village dwellers. The absence of a labor class in a western sense in the Turkish society, a country lacking the factual experience of a precise movement of industrialization, caused a break from the communications with society. As a natural and expected end, the films made in the scope of this movement slowed down after a short while. The filmatic narration tried to be established upon a social reading in conformance with Marx's social development theories was not welcomed by the Turkish public. For Özgüç the Socio-realistic Cinema ecole started with the film '*Gecelerin Ötesi (Beyond Nights)*', directed by Metin Erksan (Özgüç, 1993:103); "for the first time in the Turkish Cinema a film in real terms present[ed] a contemporary historical profile influenced even shaped by social production relations, and political-ideological character of the period" (Ufuk and Osman, 1995:11). The other exemplary film is '*Karanlıkta Uyananlar (Those Waking Up in Darkness)*', shot in 1964 by Göreç. It, too, was a film that for the first time in the Turkish Cinema history narrated the given legal rights of workers and the use of the right of syndication and strike. The film has been known with its sharp language in front a socialist perspective in a revolutionary mood. Most of these films were "metropolis films' in accordance with the highly ideological atmosphere of the era, and, narrate the stories of the city dwellers who underwent the impact of the coup at the utmost level. They were films "that were produced with an influence of communist or relatively left cinema schools" (Çokyiğit, 2010: 98), (Daldal, 2005:94-95).

Refiğ, too, indicates the close affiliation between the trend of Socio-realistic Cinema and the coup, the mentality of which was not far from socialist views: "Social Realism trend must be considered without isolating it from the 27 May issue. 27 May is one of the efforts to become westernized that failed to succeed in our history ... The first left movement in Turkish cinema in a western sense, the Social Realism trend under the influence of the West was able to develop due to the defense of the left press against the yelling and screaming of the rightist press and the noise made in the upper strata, in reality the 27 May movement never descended to the level of the public" (Refiğ, 1971:36, 38). The main common features of social realistic films crystallize as follows: i) the fact that directors at the core of the trend are directors that are politically engaged; ii) all films taking place aimed at problems of ordinary people where an open bourgeoisie meets capitalism; iii) the aesthetic and morphological innovations are eliminated; iv) the backgrounds of all these films consist of a social event rather than an individual one. Oktay dates the socio-realistic trend even back to the ideology of Kemalism noting that "The situation was put forth by Kemalism and War of Independence gets ahead of the differentiation of leftist discourse especially in cultural meaning in 1960s. Thus, divergence from the official ideology has not been made. In this sense, Kemalism gave great importance to nation formation and so national discourse has got ahead of class discourse to a great extent" (Oktay, 2000:26-27). The failure of the defenders and representatives of the socio-realistic cinema seems to be a major one as their thought of leftism had betrayed its own ideology and removed from its own nationalistic features (Türk, 2001:262). Ufuk and Osman lists some of the socio-realistic films started to develop in 1960s as follows: "Metin Erksan films: *Gecelerin Ötesi (Beyond Nights)* (1960), *Acı Hayat (The Bitter Life)* (1963), *Susuz Yaz (The Dry Summer)* (1964) and *Yılanların Öcü (The Revenge of Snakes)* (1962); Halit Refiğ films: *Yasak Aşk (The Forbidden Love)* (1961), *Şehirdeki Aşk (Love in the City)* (1963), Gurbet Kuşları *(Birds Abroad)* (1964) and Haremde Dört Kadın (*Four Women in Harem*) (1965); Ertem Gönenç film: *Karanlıkta Uyananlar (Those Waking Up in Darkness*) (1965) and Bitmeyen Yol *(The Endless Road*) (1965) directed by Duygu Sağıroğlu" (1996:10).

The Revolutionist Cinema, *Sinematek* and the Case of Yımaz Güney

Sinematek was opened in 1965 under the leadership of Onat Kutlar. Not much later, in March of 1966 *the New Cinema Journal* started to be published (Batur et all, 1985:9), both of which were considered to be the centers of the Revolutionist Cinema. Along the articles published in the journal, the essential understanding of the Revolutionist Cinema was often echoed. For example, according to Petek, one of the regular writers of the journal, "a young cinematographer is in no way an artist or cinematographer unless s/he does not call the society to a revolution with his/her cinema and camera" (Petek, 1968:6). Likewise, Onat Kutlar is quoted from the article titled "Field Survey for National Turkish Cinema" in New Cinema; October Issue, in 1967, clarifying the main anatomy of the establishment of Sinematek: "either making films that are useful to the revolution as much as current rules allow by entering into today's Turkish Cinema, or creating a revolutionary cinema market on its own by establishing production and distribution organizations completely outside of today's cinema ... Sinematek requires 'the free cinema order that does not restrict the creativity of the artist—even in personal issues' while 'not accepting the artist who does not toil to change this order as an artist." (Uçakan, 2010:83-84). Sinematek claimed to have established against traditional *Yeşilçam* patterns, most of them were conservative and unique to Turkey, together with the concepts of "localness" and "Ottomanism." Then, a group of revolutionist who started to consider Sinematek remain rather slow on the path leading to the revolution, left *Sinematek* and launched the Young Cinema Movement that would never complete its institutional structure and be doomed to remain a mere utopia. It was actually *Sinematek* which firstly showed the foreign art films in Turkey and forced the cinema funs to look beyond the national scale. Naturally, this new horizon in artistic or cultural sphere was accompanied by new social demands most of which were related to open the ways to a communist-Leninist revolution. In other words, their political ideals demanded a new conception of the socio-cultural unity of society, and in the scale of individuals, they demanded a new sense of subjectivity framed by socialist fundaments.

The fact that the 1960s were the happy years of Turkish Cinema has been a common agreement as that these years have been described by many cinema historians as the golden years of Turkish Cinema. Along these years, *Yeşilçam* movies were highly popular and constituted a considerable commercial market. As an alternative, Sinematek presented and offered the universality of cinematic art mainly exemplified by the European art cinema. This movement attracted a part of intellectuals and educated youth, only. Most of the society even did not hear from Sinematek and the literal meaning of it, let alone the artistic motives. Throughout these years, *Sinematek* would arrange organizations for the masses from the educated middle classes, intellectuals and university students. Popular discourses in *Sinematek* would circle around anti-imperialism and the utopian socialist revolution. Sinematek circle and their views were harshly criticized by the Ulusal and Milli Cinema environments. They were generally blamed for underestimating national values, trying to adopt the western values instead, ignoring the authentic values of Turkish society. For instance, Mesut Uçakan, an eminent member of Milli Cinema, argues that "the first target of the revolution [prescribed by *Sinematek* and the revolutionist cinematographers] is the radical obliteration of today's wrong cinema market, with its cliché expression, Yeşilcam and in a more general sense the complete demolition of the current order of Turkey with all its institutions in order to replace it with a Marxist one" (Uçakan, 2010:82). Likewise, Uçakan, quoted by Tosun, insistently keeps underlining the Marxist point of view of the movement (Tosun, 1992:28), as Enderun indicates the same critical trace as "they tried to present Marxism as a solution to the subconsciousness of people. All the characters (revolutionary, man of religion, worker, employer, etc.) used in their films were edited to justify the Marxist system" (Enderun, 2011:36). Refiğ, the main representative of the Ulusal Cinema ecole, even puts some names on the target and presents a quite harsh criticism asserting that "this trend[the Revolutionist Cinema] could not refrain from showing itself in cinema in its own way. The '*Young Cinema*' journal claiming to be against all the Yeşilcam's on earth, would considering a normal behavior to bark at the Turkish cinematographers; in a short time, they started to turn around and bite those who raised them such as Eczacıbaşı Cinemateque, Hisar Contests, Onat Kutlar, Atilla Dorsay and Nijat Özön" (Refiğ, 1971:160).

Yılmaz Güney's name is considered to be the only representative of the period called the 'Revolutionary Cinema' in Turkish cinema. Indicating that Yılmaz Güney's cinema established its intellectual background on a Marxist and materialist philosophy, Uçakan describes Güney's cinema as follows: "The most courageous outflow of the Marxist mentality that did not find an area of application in the Turkish cinema market in the true sense and remaining as a yearning in the minds of certain directors in theory, is doubtless Yılmaz Güney" (Uçakan, 2010:94), (Hazar, 2010:196). Yılmaz Güney set his characters and plots upon the class struggle, with a special stress on the poor and working class that's why "rural people started to see themselves on the silver screen with realistic, social realistic films and had demonstrated how much they adopted this feeling of reality with an admiration of Yılmaz Güney" (Hazar, 2010:202). However, rather than regarding his understanding of cinema, he was mostly highlighted and discussed due to his political views and his being a popular culture icon. His contributions to cinema as director, screenplay writer, actor and novelist have generally taken back seats. "Proponents of Güney—generally the leftists, [socialists and communists]—have claimed that he was a great cinematographer and that cinema [as a form of art] did not have much of a past in Turkey before him ... Those who rejected Güney—generally the right and liberals—claimed that he was a leftist and that his cinema was political and biased parallel to [his political views], [and] criticized and ignored him due to his 'lumpen' attitudes in his private life" (Hazar, 2010:204-205). "Yılmaz Güney and his films shot in 70s" automatically became a part of the arguments made around the nationalist cinema-revolutionist cinema discourses in those times, while Özgüç defines Yılmaz Güney as a charismatic personality and a history "on his own" due to his extraordinary life story and experience of cinema (Özgüç, 1993:20), (Aydın, 1997:19) (Arslan, 1997:45–48). As the pioneer of the 'Revolutionist Cinema' attempting to voice the lives staying away from the melodramas presented within the westernization policies of the official ideology, Güney tried in a way to place ordinary lives against this view in a Marxist-Leninist way, that's why 'Revolutionary Cinema' is mostly limited to Güney films.

Arrested in 1972, Güney went into jail and gained a 'class-based perspective' there, which played a vital role on that he would display the revolutionist ideology in a stronger way along his films after all. He describes this bitter experience as "a process of learning of the Marxist-Leninist revolution and revisionism" (Güney, 2000:63) (Güney, 2003:11). Again, he is quoted to have declared along an article he penned as "[the] true judge is the public. But when we say public, the opinion that the public now has cannot be fully meant. The opinion that the public currently carries holds the ideology of the ruling powers of the past and of today" (Uçakan, 2010:94). For Refiğ, on the other hand, he does not only act in front of the camera but also in the real life since he becomes "populist if people are mentioned, socialist if labor is mentioned, existentialist if humanism is mentioned, Maoist if the revolution is discussed, able to get along with all groups that are in conflict with each other, claiming to be patriotic when it is fitting, anarchist when it is fitting, the attitude of the ugly king is the typical appearance of archivism that has become chronic" (Refiğ, 1971:156). Presenting a feminist stance, Dönmez celebrates Güney since "unlike traditional Turkish rural melodramas that set up the narrative around the highest-ranking male member of the family, usually the father who maintains the patriarchal ideology, the films of Güney show the collapse of such a system" (Dönmez-Colin, 2004:51).

The film *Umut* (Hope), shot by Yılmaz Güney in 1970, stands as a milestone for Güney's filmography as it was considered by those inclining to socialistic-communistic views as "the most advanced, most daring, most revolutionary, most activist work of art of Turkish Cinema" (Gökmen, 1973b:122). Battal, for instance, modifies the film as "the presentation of the real face of reality in a multi-dimensional manner" (2006:201), which seems to have been uttered just for the sake of eulogizing the film, nothing more. Arslan, too, displays an exaggerated stance noting that "*Umut* is a radical turn for both Turkish Cinema and the cinema of Güney. The looking distance in Güney's subsequent films to the integral nation symbol, and the style of narration that removes the look from the phantasmic frame of the nation will appear in front of us" (2010:354). The approach of Giovanni Scognamillo, a master of the history of Turkish Cinema, stands to be quite realistic and balanced as he regards *Umut* as "Güney's first film of quest in terms of context, form and interpretation" (2003:323). Güney seems to have strived to display with *Umut* that ordinary people mostly lack the power to change the reality of life, the metaphysical values or beliefs. And, attempts to change them are doomed to become in vain. Unlike the popular exaggerations, Uçakan asserts, "Umut did not draw any box office and met with the public's interest ... Yılmaz has not yet made any films in the name of the labor class" (Uçakan, 2010:101,103,112). Analyzing opposite criticism, Refiğ declares that he did not like *Umut* at all "since the drama tried to be created in the film was foreign to him. A horse cart driver in Adana loses his horse and no one helps him to find his horse. He remains completely alone. That was against the social structure and social relations that he researched and felt an interest in Turkey" (Türk, 2001:290). Besides, "the best parts of the film are these first scenes that are limited only to observations. Then an accident happens, one of the horses of the coachman dies. Starting with this scene, the film stops being an observationist and starts to make comments on the structure of Turkish society and human behavior. These comments have no relation to the structural reality of the Turkish society and the film consists only of an outer appearance of realism occurring due to the fact that it was shot in natural locations because of the efforts to adapt the western social structure and humane behaviors randomly into the story" (Refiğ, 1971:152). For Uçakan, the case is not too much different, his criticism is mostly focused on the way Güney approaches Islam and the religious figure in the film: "*Umut* assesses everything from a materialistic angle ... He attempted to describe the inadequacy of this order. However, he could not get away from clearly making it felt that he exaggerated events and that he shaped them in accordance with his own interpretation with fake characters. It cannot be said that he acted in real manner when considering religion. The types that he portrays as representatives of religion were people who corrupted Islam from the inside, who are actually enemies of religion and behaviors that he showed as religious motives such as fortune telling and giving news of some other worlds were in fact actions that the religion of Islam strongly rejects" (Uçakan, 2010:96-97). In sum, the criticism posed to the Yılmaz Güney-revolutionist Cinema has been centered on the general view that it misread the social structure of the Turkish society by reducing the socio-economic problems of the country to just a class struggle, as it took place in the Western societies.

12 September 1980-1990: Marching Boots Leading to the Tunnel of Horror

Along the dark hours of September 12th, 1980, the democratic life in Turkey was intervened second time by the military junta. Their excuse for that illegal and illegitimate coup d'état was not much different from the one asserted for the coup realized in 1960.In reality, the coup of 12 September 1980 did basically mean a big blow on democracy, human rights, freedom of thought, culture and art in Turkey. As Tachau and Heper argue, "the military's claim that the 1980 coup saved Turkey's political democracy from civil war also bolstered its increased power," and "this claim was made in a military culture and a society that [did not do much more than] legitimiz[ing] the military's historical mission and institutional political role as the guardian of the state, and it supported a new pattern of increased military influence" (Tachau and Heper, 1983:162). Heper argues, that "the 1982 Constitution made reference to 'Turkish historical and moral values'. This was a fundamental 'deviation' from the original Atatürkian approach, according to which the consciousness of the new Turk was to be rooted in science" (1991:49-50). The fact "the military has used legal/ constitutional, historical/cultural, and structural reasons and mechanisms to retain its privileged position in issuing demands, policy suggestions, and warnings on political matters" (Tachau and Heper, 1983:153) was mostly interpreted as a direct support to the right wing of the politics in Turkey by Kaplan and Cizre as they claim that "the military leaders have most often associated themselves with the right-of-center political spectrum-most notably, the religious sponsors of the 'Turkish-Islamic synthesis' ideology" (Kaplan, 2002:114), (Cizre, 2005:24-28). The years following the coup gradually became a term when political and ideological oppressions increased, labor unions decreased and the poverty became widespread, as natural result of the intervention of democratic life.

As of the intellectuals and intellectual and artistic thought, "the coup brought about a tremendous regression and introversion ... the ideological transformation made the intellectual lose his/her ideals. While old ideals were replaced by being favored in the market and the quest for popularity, the intellectual started to see no harm to in considering the bourgeoisie as the main support unit, without getting by upon a social base" (Bostan and Atam, 2006:136). Between 1985 and 1995, "consumerism was the rising ideology that alone determined the cultural environment of 80s.The Turkish Cinema could not find theatres to run its films as American film companies opened their own offices in Turkey and were able to run their films in Turkey simultaneously with other countries. Turkish films mostly dealt with social events and personal identity crisis. Kongar is quoted "describing that new identity of *Yeşilçam* trying to become different" as that he has "no doubt about that quest for identity has been impressed by cultural elements, ideological factors and the new world view ... And this anxiety of identity quest has not been free from the anxiety of identity quest of the general Turkish culture" (Güçhan, 1992:95). Maktav attracts attentions to another dramatic point while he declares that "along the process between 80s and 90s, poverty stopped being a problematic issue in Turkish Cinema. The fact that the poor started to be considered out of the classes in the society has been one of the ways of manifestations of the post-modern life upon the screen" (Maktav, 2004:990). The [Turkish] cinema of 80s was recognized as the "cinema of depression" (Erdoğan, 1999:122), naturally parallel to the depoliticization process brought by the coup. Uçakan notes that it was an era when "ideologies were banned, thinking intellectuals were tortured in prisons, the people were increasingly becoming cosmopolitan and secular, and the culture of indifference and fun were dominant. It can be said that our cinema [the entire Turkish Cinema] has been left out of control at this time (Uçakan, 2007:230).

As a natural output, the films shot along the era of the coup, were contextually far from the political and social criticism. Films—that were mostly produced by mere individual efforts—were modified by the military junta as 'films against state', and banned. Porno films of 70s were replaced by arabesque-singer-melodramas, and films dealing with social problems left their places to those handling with individual crisis. The situation was so dramatic that "the military coup swept away the political cinema that had been quite established; instead, films of frustration and arabesque have taken over" (Hazar, 2010:216). Most of the directors of that time have become gradually introvert and narrated their own selves and made films focusing on their own ideologies and despairs which were not welcomed by the cinema audience. In other words, "these films remained as films of incomprehensible pains, defeat and intimidation, which could do nothing other than giving nihilist messages. In the post-1980 Turkish cinema when even the films about 12 September could not directly target the state, regime, politicians (this is of course partly due to the censorship, yet at time same time, still is a matter of position), on the contrary identified themselves with the mentality 12 September aimed to create, intention to fight for a humanist, democratic, just social order which would be created with left values became meaningless" (Maktav, 2000:87-88).

"12 September films," which generally narrated the terror before 1980, the oppression era of the 12 September coup, the dramatic position of the people who put in prison, stayed in jail for long, and found the society and community relations totally changed after their service, could only be shot long after the era of coup due to the fears of prosecution. The socio-psychological pressures of the 12 September regime have been endeavored to be narrated along these films via the terror before 12 September, the struggle of the right and left, the problems originating from ideological polarizations, characters who were involved in generally left organizations before 1980. Surprising enough, those on the right who suffered as much as the leftists from the tortures and prosecutions of the coup have been quite indifferent to reflect their agony on the screen. A heavy pessimism and dark despair are the dominant elements along the films. "Coup" alone has never been presented as the main factor causing all the agony; but rather, they have preferred to tell the stories emphasizing the psycho-social impacts of coup in a rather indirect way. It could simply be asserted that the cultural and artistic imagination scope of the whole country, and this scope's ideological and imaginary content were redesigned during and after the coup. The stress and tonation were transformed to the state from the individual, highlighting traditions and dogmatic norms instead of free thought and artistic creativity. For Tümay, those films were nothing but "the replacements of the anger towards the social power that prevents self-indicted punishment by overcoming the subject's own limits and restrictions by moving into the psychic sound and the feeling of guilt" (Arslan, 2010:288). The outstanding 12 September films could be listed as follows, though their number might be increased taking minor references: Mesut Uçakan's *Öç* (1984), Sinan Çetin's *Prenses* (1986), Şerif Gönen's *Sen Türkülerini Söyle* (1986), Zeki Ökten *Ses* (1986), Zeki Alasya's *Dikenli Yol* (1986), Yavuz Özkan's *Yağmur Kaçakları* (1987), Şerif Gönen's *Sen de Yüreğinde Sevgiye Yer Aç* (1987), Ali Özgentürk's *Su Da Yanar* (1987), Melih Gülgen's *Kimlik* (1988), Erdal Kıral's *Av Zamanı* (1988), Memduh Ün's *Bütün Kapılar Kapalıydı* (1989), Muammer Özer's *Kara Sevdalı Bulut* (1989), Ümit Efekan's *Darbe* (1990), Zülfü Livaneli's *Sis* (1989), İrfan Tözüm's *İkili Oyunlar* (1990), Tomris Giritlioğlu's *Suyun Öte Yanı* (1991), Oğuzhan Tercan's *Uzlaşma* (1991), Atıf Yılmaz's *Bekle Dedim Gölgeye* (1991), Candan Evcimen İçöz's *Hoşçakal Umut* (1993), Yusuf Kurçenli's *Çözülmeler* (1994), Tomris Giritlioğlu's *80. Adım* (1995), Handan İpekçi's *Babam Askerde* (1994), Osman Sınav's *Gerilla* (1995), İsmail Güneş's *Gülün Bittiği Yer* (1998), Atıf Yılmaz's *Eylül Fırtınası* (1999), Yılmaz Erdoğan's *Vizontele Tuuba* (2003), Çağan Irmak's *Babam ve Oğlum* (2005), Ömer Uğur's *Eve Dönüş* (2006), Sırrı Süreyya Önder ve Muharrem Gülmez's *Beynelmilel* (2006), Atıl İnaç's *Zincirbozan* (2007).

After 90's: Same Old Same Old, towards a New Millennium

The years between 1983 and 1991 are mostly considered to be the period when the values of consumerism gradually rose up along the

Turkish Cinema. The newly-emerging middle class produced by consumerism and neo-liberalism were dominantly represented in varying forms throughout the Turkish Cinema. For Miyasoğlu, this term, the end of 80's, refers to a time when "cinematographers produced films that were focused on award juries with the incentives they received from the Ministry of Culture, as they were unable to do anything else except for displaying the frustrations of small bourgeois intellectuals. Keeping up this irresponsibility throughout the 90's, they perhaps chose intellectual suicide" (Miyasoğlu, 2010:162). Evren, on the other hand, define[s] "the year of 1987 as a time of change-transformation in the history of Turkish Cinema based on the concrete data at hand ... [as] capital owners and persons [came] from different channels but who wished to produce a cinema with their own means fill[ed] the vacancy in the Turkish Cinema during the 1994's, and a new period called the *independents* started in Turkish cinema with radical structuring that have no ties to previous terms" (Evren, 2010:53,57). The emergence of Commercial TV channels was another dramatic factor influencing the course of the Turkish Cinema in 90s: "from around the mid-1990s onwards ... at the turn of the new millennium—a moment when commercial television has entered into 99 per cent of homes—Turkish Cinema has acquired a second breath of life (Kerslake et.al., 2010:397). On the other hand, things did not come up roses, as expected. Evren argues that "the Turkish Cinema after 90s both created radical changes in its language and started to displayed many taboos and endeavored to transform the general, ages-old views of the society. However, this efforts were not welcomed by the society in general and that's why the Turkish Cinema in 90s was modified as a cinema in crisis" (Evren, 1994). Likewise, Güven notes that the dominance of Hollywood decreased the number of the audience seeing the native films at a dramatic level since "only 33 films were shot in 1991 and only 15 of them could have the chance to be run" (Güven, 2004:28).

The Turkish Cinema emerging after 90s has generally been called as "The New Turkish Cinema," defined as a cinema that "put the crisis of identity and belonging in Turkey crystallizing gradually since 90s on the agenda and argued in the frame of varying cinematical, philosophical and ideological stances" (Suner, 2004:257). The practitioners of this new trend have been a new generation trying to compose their own language and make the art of cinema their life philosophy. This generation has mostly been educated on cinema, followed film festivals abroad, lived there and mingled their lives entirely with the art of cinema, who have left the narration traditions of Yeşilçam aside and preferred rather plain and restrained themes and narrative techniques: "A generation of young directors appeared some of whom were interns at Yeşilçam, with others trained at cinema schools ... through the economic and political status of Turkey rising in the eyes of the world during the 2000's and the "general" stability in domestic politics caused the cinema sector to meet new names ... such as Zeki Demirkubuz, Nuri Bilge Ceylan, Reha Erdem, Derviş Zaim" (Şen, 2010:28,30).

Regarding the situation of 'the Conservative Turkish Cinema', Yavuz claims that "new opportunity spaces in the market have allowed Muslim actors to carve their own space, among other things through their own movies, novels, poetry, music" (2009:58). In a meeting titled as 'Visual Arts and Islam', organized by ISAV (Islamic Research Foundation) at the beginning of 90s, the affiliation among art, religion and ideology was expressed by the motto "art is for the sake of Islam" (Özek, et al., 2003:18). For Özdemir, likewise, "the Islamist cinema trend containing narrations with religious themes at the center, gain[ed] popularity in 1990's when political parties defining themselves with an Islamic identity started to put this aspect of them forward... [However], the Islamic Cinema [gave] the first signs that it ha[d] left behind its activist attitude with the new products coming out in 2005" (2011:8). A political discourse became evidently dominant along the Conservative Turkish Cinema, which offered a more conservative life style parallel to the conservative developments in Turkey. But "this new cinema unlike the old, is becoming apolitical, its ideological borders are increasingly being dulled at this time" (Uçakan, 2007:155). Some of the examples of the Turkish Conservative Cinema are as follows: *Yalnız Değilsiniz* (1) (1990), *Sonsuza Yürümek* (1992), *Sevdaların Ölümü* (1992), *Yalnız Değilsiniz (2)* (1992), *İskilipli Atıf Hoca* (1993), *Kelebekler Sonsuza Uçar* (1993), *Ölümsüz Karanfiller* (1995), *Minyeli Abdullah (2)* (1990), *Kurdoğlu* (1991), *Bir Zamanlar Sarhoştu* (1992), *Kanayan Yara*

Bosna (1994), *Bosna Mavi Karanlık* (1994), *Beşinci Boyut* (1993), *Bize Nasıl Kıydınız* (1994).

The Turkish Cinema in and after 2000s, an obvious individualism has been standing out, the framework of which has been shaped by the main principles of the author cinema. As Hazar notes, "it [is the] time to make individual cinema and—at best—catch some local dialects over the director cinema" (2010:237). Şen celebrates a parallel development as he argues that "in 2009, 69 films were run in Turkey. The general picture of the 2000's shows that mostly domestic productions lead in the most watched 10 films and that most of the list consists of Turkish films" (Şen, 2010:31). Doğan underlines the financial support coming from Euroimages "29.34 million French francs between 1997 and 2000," as a contribution to the author cinema and "the production of "art films" (Doğan, 2010:41, 42). Güneş, on the other hand, links the positive response of the Turkish and international audience towards new Turkish films to "tell[ing] eastern stories and talk[ing] about feelings little known by westerners" (Güneş, 2010:67). Miyasoğlu, on the other hand, draws a rather pessimistic outline:

> Our cinema is now standing in the stalemate of these two types of films and is trying to way out for itself. On the one hand, the films of known celebrities in show business breaking box office records, gathering audiences with a certain humor, seeing its own fantasies to be more important than all the concerns of our cinema and not caring about any moral concerns for success without any limitations ... On the other hand, art films moving with a slow pace with aesthetic concerns without taking the audience into account, trying to give credit to every frame while telling the story of the film, challenging the patience of the audience and collecting the votes of cinema juries with surprising innovations. (2010:164).

Turkish Cinema has been suffering from a sever censorship mechanism since its emerging years. Uçakan argues that "according to still valid rules of censorship system set up in 1923 for Turkish cinema and undergoing very few changes, a film performing the following actions is either banned or is permitted to be shown by removing the scenes containing criminal elements:

1. Performing the political, economic or civilian propaganda of any state
2. Offending the feelings of friendly nations and governments
3. Conducting religious propaganda
4. Conducting ideological propaganda
5. Violating general morals, ethics and national feelings
6. Conducting propaganda to offend the honor of the military, against military forces
7. Containing scenes to be tooled of propaganda against Turkey (Uçakan, 2007:276).

The Regulations Regarding the Control of Films and Film Scenarios dated 1939 originating from the Police Duties Authority Law dated 1939, has remained in force for years until the Cinema, Video and Music Works Law numbered 3257 ratified in 1986. These regulations containing very general and rounded provisions have been softened and hardened from time to time, regarding to the changes of political power and the ideological stances of the members of the Censure Board. This is not surprising for Esen as "the political culture in Turkey carried conformist characteristics in the majority; attachment to authority and conformism is one of the leading features of political culture in Turkey. The concepts such as 'opposing' and 'criticism' do not exist in our political culture. This factor is effective on the autocensorship issue in the cinema ... Either official censorship or the censorship that is the forcing of the economic dimension of cinema, in conclusion prevent the projection on the screen of a real social evening-up in Turkey" (Esen, 2000:174-175). There have been tragicomical applications along the censorship history of Turkish Cinema Turkish Cinema could not get rid of censorship quite a while. The censorship that was applied on cinema in 1939 maintained its effectiveness after 27 May movement too. Struggles to repeal this legislation remained inconclusive. This effectiveness of censorship has been prevented cinema to be a real industry. Interesting enough, "only the art of cinema in Turkey is controlled by the administrative force of political authority in two stages before the work of art is produced, constantly after it is produced and this time constantly by the judicial forces (Batur et all, 1985:24).

"Each film more or less bears an ideology."

Giovanni Scognamillo

Instead of an Epilogue

Ben-Ghiat asserts that "rapid technological change, shifting boundaries between public and private spheres, and the advent of mass consumerism raised anxieties among intellectuals that cut across confines of ideology as well as geography" (1996:110). Accordingly, the artist—any artist—has been realizing an interactive relationship with almost all forms of artistic creation and esthetical ideologies, and, s/he has been exposed to motives of a/dominant environmental conditions, which is not a kind of socio-psychological complex or a form chaos but the very essence of the nature. Ideology embraces our social life by its cultural dimension (Culler, 1973:481), and "ideology is made the measure of art, and artist and audience are seen as integrated in an organism, the total state" (Dworkin, 1977:98), (Koçer 483). The fact that "the film-image is, however managed and distorted by direction, editing, or projection itself, a real image, an art not of mediation but of witness (and witness) by both filmmaker and viewer, something to be seen, with the same immediacy and compelling factuality as the sights and sounds of the "real" world (McConnell, 1972:545-546) underlies its ideological effect and makes it become a kind of "mass-cultural hieroglyphics," Adorno argues, [that] "prevent[s] human beings from changing, from being different, from distinguishing their own wishes and needs from those imposed upon them by distribution from above" (Hansen, 1992:51-52). Pandian asserts that "there is something deeply ideological in the association of cinema with temporal contingency in modern times," and asks "is the relationship between cinema, time and freedom no more than a chapter in the history of ideology?" (2011:194). In a replying way, Rothman considers that the common webs of theories neglect the sense of "work of art" and seek desperately for an ideological dimension and claim for it along films as "conflicting, dogmatic and doctrinal" (2004). For Chapman, on the other hand, the fact that "film theorists who, inspired by Marxist cultural studies, have been obsessed with exposing the ideological and aesthetic conservatism of classical Hollywood cinema (2003:36), since "the conclusion Marxist theorists reached was that capitalism, through its mass popular art industry—the movies, TV, radio, popular music, and so on—confuses, mystifies, and manipulates our minds in such a way as to thwart the development of ... the Capitalist subject who believes himself to be an autonomous, unified, free agent is really dominated" (Carroll, 1988:53,58), (Prince, 1996:35), (Sobchack, 1997:5). "Western semiotics," too, is blamed to be mistaken as the Marxist theorists, since "[it] as a deciphering operation, not only dismisses the 'obvious' and the 'habitual' as false consciousness but also sets out to marginalize competing ideological interpretation" (Teshome, 1986:144).

Zimmer claims there is no innocent film, it could be asserted, no film without some political incidence (1974:123-124), as Wood modifies the features of a typical ideological film regarding three worldwide known films: *Battleship Potemkin, Triumph of the Will* and *Vent d'Est*, "they have one thing in common: none of them permits the spectator, within the work, an alternative view to the one promulgated by the film-maker (1976:44). That is, ideology seems to have been at work in many ways and aspects when cinematic art is in concern, though this stance should not be defined as a law of cinematic criticism. Verifying the close affiliation between film art and ideology, Dorsay speaks rather sure stating that "a film is a product of a certain world view as any work of art and in regard to every world view rests on a certain ideology; to some extent every film is located in the frame of an ideology" (Dorsay 1984:70), while "the ideological and institutional role of the cinematic apparatus ... as an imprinting machine" (Rosen, 1981:8) and "the ideological demands made of entertainment" (Rosenbaum, 1997:3) make obvious the "extraordinary power of conviction" of cinematic art (Resina, 1998:68). To get rid of the negative aspects of that power, "film have to be "read" to uncover the ideological assumptions implicit in their narrative trajectories, [keeping in mind that] at the same time there are inherent limits to the directness and forcefulness with which it can be successfully deployed" (Green, 1993:111-112). Dittmar also offers "a methodology, a way of reading film "language" as a repository of politics and ideology" against cinematic manipulation (1995:43). The problem facing the affiliation between the film theory and ideology is described as that "the challenge for film theory is to find a method of conceptualizing the presence and place of ideology within cultural products that does not result in a unidirectional communicational process, flattening and rendering passive spectatorial activity" (Prince, 1988:30).

To label a film as ideological "necessarily entails an antagonistic relationship of critic to work and establishes what amount to either/or parameters on the range of meanings attributable to the work in question" (Poague, 1985:31), and, "contemporary social formations cannot be adequately given through cinema . . .and the present assumption that the ideological nature of social constructions (of 'society') can be the problematic around and through which a film operates, is incorrect" (Gidal, 1979:77). In addition, the governmental and national interests have always been intervened into cinematic creation as "no major film company, without the sanction of national policy, was bold enough to treat the subject of dictatorships and their aggressive atrocities, or the growing expansion of their ideological adherents" (Jacobs, 1967:1), which brings about a panorama of that "the category of "World Cinema" proves on closer inspection to be less "natural," less ideologically innocent" (Roberts, 1998:77). On the other hand, The facts that the audience reception has never been measured precisely and objectively (Maltby, 1984:49), and, that the audience sometimes might not receive the ideological messages embedded as expected or reject them totally (Green, 1993:125-126) put questions marks to the issue of determining ideological ends for films. Cooper handles the issue from a varying point of view asserting that "film ideology is less a problem of how the spectator looks at the film than of how moving images have looked at their spectators" (1998:109) since "film today plays a significant role in articulating and perpetuating what might be called global mythologies: ideological discourses about the world and humanity's relationship to it" (Roberts, 1998:62). However, "in the ideological superstructure of an evolving consumer society" (Taylor, 1996:28), the alternatives do not seem to be much in number "if ideology is all around us," [as] "we can no longer measure resistance and the struggle for change along the yardstick of a non-ideological reality" (O'Shea and Schwarz, 1987:108). No matter "the function of cinema, within capitalist ideology, is the 'perpetual retotalisation of the imaginary'" (Buckland, 1989:95), "research on cinema ... has emphasized the necessity of a non-reductive approach to cinema and ideology (Klinger, 1997:122).

Re-reading Kemalist Ideology and Turkish Modernization Story: Attacking to the Past for Favoring the New

There have been two basic ideological eras along the contemporary Turkish history: the emergence period of Kemalism and the 60s. Both of the eras bear the dominance of "the pressure of extreme secularism," and, "this brings on the mandatory secularization of the public area ... All kinds of religious symbols and organizing are placed under pressure. The public domain in today's Turkey is under the guardianship of the state, which is imposing a secular lifestyle through authoritarian methods" (Göle, quoted by Kuru: 2011:16). Positivism and materialism have been so much affective that Turkey became a country of "social laboratory [and] an experiment" (Karpat, 2011:131), and of "a positivistic mausoleum" (Adıvar, 1947:279). Whereas Kongar relates the crisis of culture and ideology in Turkey to that "the ideology transferred from abroad was not contributed by the technology that bore it, and the Turkish-Islamic society did not succeed to produce their own ideology" (Kongar, 1999:372), Armağan points out as the fundamental cause the ignorance of the traditional culture and assessing it "as an element that set an obstacle against modernization" for the sake of "a full realization of westernization" (1999:87). Göle and Magnarella, in a varying mode declare the same crucial point, the rejection of the Islamic past (Göle, 1997a:167), (Magnarella, 1970:229).

Yakup K. Karaosmanoğlu, the outstanding novelist of the Republican era, and a devoted supporter of M. Kemal and his revolutions, coined "the term "Kemalism" on 28 June 1929 to refer to the new nation and state-building ideology that defined the legitimate political vocabulary constituting the basic principles and values of the Turkish path to modernity. Then the term "Kemalism" was used in the mainstream historiography of the Turkish Revolution to refer to a new political stand that interpreted the revolutionary practices that had taken place between 1923 and 1935 within the framework of the tradition of ideological positivism ... Ali Kazancıgil argued that Kemalist ideology was an amalgam of the ideas associated with laicism, nationalism, solidarist positivist political theory, and 19th-century scientism" (İrem, 2002:87). Saktanber, too, confirms that "Kemalism is the ideology ... used as an ideological guideline by the republican regime ... Kemalism has continued to be a framework of thought for intellectuals who even today follow in Atatürk's path" (2006:24). Kushner, on the other hand, displays a somewhat opposing stance noting that "the period of Mustafa Kemal Atatürk, following the final dissolution of the Empire, ultimately enabled Turkism to become a political doctrine. The Kemalists did not produce an ideology in the strict sense, but their statements and actions did point to some definite directions" (1997:222). Rustow modifies the Kemalist ideology as a "corporatist ideology that sees the nation as an amalgamated mass lacking priorities and social classes," such an ultra-utopian approach that even utopia writers along the world literature could not figure out (1973:102). Moderate enough, Kaya summarizes Kemalist ideology in short: "adopting 'modern' civilization, stressing Turkish culture and making Islam a [mere] matter of personal conviction (2004:63), and points out the logic processed along the revolutions as that the Kemalists "argued that the Turkish republic could not be content with gradual evolutionary progress, but that, in contrast, the process of modernization had to be speeded up by revolutionary measures" (2004:80). For Ahmad, issues are not too much different since "the first step was expected to lead the creation of a totally new society, and for such a society they knew they had to create 'a new type of Turk very different from the Ottoman'" (Ahmad, 1993:77). As of the revolutionary reforms, Kadıoğlu asserts that "these reforms constituted an onslaught on the existing cultural practices. They opted for a general state of amnesia which would lead to a process of estrangement of the people from some of their own cultural practices ... The 1920s and the 1930s were crucial years in the making of the new Republican Turkey and the emergence of the 'new Turks'" (1996:186). That is, "modernization in [Turkey] has been basically a state project implemented by the reformist elite" (Şafak, 2006:24).

The picture is not difficult to describe: "the Turkish rejection of their imperial past was at once an ideology, a policy, and a mood" (Lewis, 1980:33), "the principle of the welfare and existence of the nation, that is, the driving force of the culture policies between 1923-1950 brings to the agenda the uniform and pure national culture theory ... The principle of nationalism and contemporization creating the codes of the Atatürk period culture policy taking as a basis the survival of the state determines its contents along creating a homogenous society in the control of the government" (Öndin, 2003:56,57,60), "it was definite that the Turkish nationalism that broke off from its past in order to meet a future without traditions, would become the dominant ideology of the new state established in Anatolia" (Cündioğlu, 2005: 24), (Erdemir, 2006:383). As Spencer remarkably points out, "the party of Atatürk found rational justification in an ideology which, although imported, permitted a course of nationalist action" (Spencer, 1958:640), which brought about an inevitable culture shift caused by "a process of breaking off from culture and moving toward non-culture or 'ideology'" (Aksoy, 1989:5), (Demir, 2004:31), (Feldman, 1991:100). The fact that "nationalism was not only emphasized as a principle, but was written into the constitution as inseparable from the nature of the Turkish Republic (Kaya, 2004:151), since "the Westernist cadre that founded the Republic of Turkey did not stop at just eliminating the sultanate, they also targeted Islamic institutions that they regarded as the second leg of the traditional old order, in other words, *the past era*" (Kuru, 2011:228). As a natural result of this stress on nationalism, "like other agencies of popular socialization, a national cinema [became] a vehicle for a 'common culture and a civic ideology, a set of common understandings and aspirations, sentiments and ideas, that binds the population together in their homeland'" (Smith, 1991:11).

The general position of the country shaped by nationalistic and positivistic doctrines transformed to such extremities that the republican Turkish Cinema could simply be asserted to be a cinema of a purely propaganda cinema, intent on ideological control and indoctrination as "attacking religion [basically Islam], religious people and religious values, demeaning and ridiculing them; confronting us at various occasions in Turkish cinema [was] a common attitude ... On the one hand there are Kuvay-ı Milliye (national forces) who want[ed] to save the country, on the other hand there [were] traitorous men of religion who [did] not want the country to be saved, who [were] enemies of the National Struggle" (Lüleci, 2009:39,40). Öztürk discloses the same republican propaganda-indoctrination task through cinematic art with specific documents:

> Süreyya Pasha indicated that he believed cinema and theater should exist in every civilized country as they serve to the education and morals of the public, took the side of those who wanted to open the way for both these arts. In his bill, Süreyya Pasha had explained in detail in which positive services cinema had been used for until 1930. The contributions made to national education had been primarily emphasized with the adjective 'very substantial'. Cinema had made more of a contribution than the press for the Alphabet Revolution. While newspapers had a daily circulation of forty or fifty thousand, the number of spectators reached by cinemas was at least 'half a million' per day. Looking at this statistical information obtained by Süreyya Pasha, whose source we do not know, the half a million people reached by cinemas 'had learned the new alphabet''. According to the emphasis in the offer, cinema and theater were also a 'major tool of propaganda scientifically, socially and politically'. The political authority should benefit from this propaganda tool as 'a branch of national education'. (2005:142).

Particular films were shot during the initial years of the Republic so that the public should digest the forms of westernization faster and easier. An obvious pro-westernization attitude was portrayed and visualized along the films such as *Kubilay, Çalıkuşu, Ateşten Gömlek.* Presented as representatives of modernization and development, teachers, doctors or engineers were juxtaposed against mostly ecclesiastics, and representatives of traditional local authorities, such as clan chiefs or village elders. Islam was criticized as a metaphysical focus of authority.

Odd enough, while almost all melodramas shot along the republican era were designed and expected to be transfer vehicles of the values of westernization, they would fully confirm and glorify the traditional positions of the family, the woman and man, in an utmost patriarchal manner. "Females became means of Kemalist movement along both civilization project and ideology of nationalism" (Göle, 1997b:90). the first movie star of republican Turkish Cinema, Cahide Sonku, for instance, was strongly celebrated and glorified by the republican elites as she was "blonde," not a typical Anatolian brunet (Büker, 2002:153). Sonku's importance was not only attributed to her western body and outlook but also to her being Turkey's first female director and producer: "she looked like the westernized woman that the republic ideology describes. Audience named her as our [their] Greta Garbo" (Büker and Uluyağcı, 1993:19). That is, the women of republican Turkish Cinema were considered to be "markers of secularism, engineers as transmitters of positivism and rationality, and intellectuals incarnating" (Rustow, 1973:102) (Dorsay, 1985:97). In addition to this tragic abuse of female figures, Turkish Cinema has been blamed to prefer an ideological stance against women since "it has drawn woman models in line with the power relations of the paternal order and requirements of ideology ... In order to legitimize these inequalities and to soften the daily tensions of female spectators, life and social relationships were reestablished in a way to be described as 'inevitable' through films" (Abisel, 2005:136). Female figures in popular republican Turkish films had ever been dressed in the way to conform to the dress-code revolutions and their attitudes were also designed in accordance with reformations. Their place in society, too, has been interestingly defined around the traditional duties and responsibilities, unlike the common western ways: "The traditional status of women in society follows a line that is based for young girls to transition to marriage and at the end to being a grandmother, based on the 'natural life cycle'. The woman is deprived of individual choice and political power throughout her life" (Göle, 2000:120).

Post 60s have mostly been considered to be the era when the actual ideological fraction on Turkish cinematic intellectuality took place. To underline this fact, Oskay declares that "till 60s, the Turkish tradition of cinema had been remained as a mere cinema of escape, lingering and manipulation" (Oskay, 1996:98). It was that era when socialism and communism entered the intellectual and academic circles in an effective way and impressed artists and masses at a certain extent due to the chaotic political and economic situation of the country. Nazım Hikmet, the legendary communist poet who "provided a "cultural, ideological, reflective, and...theory-forming response to modernization" (Soja, 1989: 29)—he pasted his last days in Communist Russia and died there—spoke on art in those days as "I believe that writers, communist writers in particular, must create a literature which will become one of the sources of knowledge of real life...I would like to write poems, novels, plays which had this virtue for my people and for other peoples" (Hikmet et al., I964:357-8) (Karpat, 1966:175). The intellectual stance of the leftist youth of post 60s that cherished most of the cinematographists, who put the layers of the Turkish Cinema after 60s, was not too much different from Hikmet's ideological approach. According to their belief, "the "duty" of youth [was] to dedicate their lives to the construction of a future society, whether envisioned as the recuperation of the early Kemalist period, a socialist utopia" (Neyzi, 2001:420). Furthermore, Özdemir notes:

> students who were inspired by TİP [The Turkish Labor Party] and its sympathizers' radical section founded Revolutionist Youth Federation (DEV-GENÇ) in 1969 at Ankara. Türkiye Halk Kurtuluş Ordusu (Turkey Public Army of Salvation) (THKO) lead by Deniz Gezmiş, Türkiye Halk Kurtuluş Cephesi (Turkey Public Salvation Front) (THKP-C) lead by Mahir Çayan and Türkiye İhtilalci İşçi Köylü Partisi (Turkey Revolutionist Labor-Villager Party) lead by Doğu Perinçek which then evolved to TKP-ML (Turkey Marxist-Leninist Communist Party) were born via various ideological, organizational and leadership debates within the process and in 1970s they generated derivatives with several fractions up to fifty. When the year 1970 came, student movement in general, leadership of socialist action's ideological and actual in private came under the rule of

> Marxist-Leninist groups that wanted to be organized as armed action unions and defended armed campaigns. (1995:226).

Most of the films of this period—i.e. *Vurun Kahpeye* (Refiğ, 1973), *Hudutların Kanunu* (Akad, 1966), *Çalıkuşu* (Seden, 1966)—had directly or indirectly propagated the ideological stance advocating that 'the local-traditional-religious values are obstacles standing in the way of modernization'. As a matter of fact, the modernization and social transformation policies of the official ideology were fully adopted along the production process of those films. This tragicomic position is assessed by Nezih Erdoğan as that "the Turkish popular cinema describes a national identity," which remains quite irrelevant and inadequate to clarify the axioms of the era (Erdoğan, 1998:262). Another puzzling development in the era was the dramatic failure and inconsistency that *Ulusal* Cinema could not get rid of. That is, '*Ulusal* Cinema' was initiated with the purpose of celebrating the public-traditional and religious—values and to develop a cinema language conforming to this end. However, most of the films shot along this period re/presented the outstanding social figures as the pioneers of modernization (teachers, doctors, lawyers, etc.) who had ceaselessly fought against the tradition and religion. Traditional and religious values were again portrayed as the main obstacles preventing so-called modernization and its derivative components.

Collins relates the place of ideology in artistic creation to the conditions brought by postmodernity as that "the future of ideological analysis depends on how we come to terms with postmodernism since it problematizes so thoroughly our critical assumptions about cultural production" (1987:11). This crucially significant situation automatically conditions "the death of the author and artist" since "the reader and audience have as much say so over the text as its creator" (Cündioğlu, 2013:169). The so-called post-modern cinema, in the same vein, displays three elements unified in a single body, a schizophrenic experience, a psychopathic indifference and an undefined sense of quest which has been ideologized to the largest extent with an abnormal view of nihilism. This sad and problematic position of today's post-modern cinema understanding is blamed by Sam of "caus[ing] the creation of a consumption ideology that is made attractive" since it is this cinema that "prepares the grounds suitable for triggering interaction with its effect in complex team processes due to themes that are different from one another" (Sam, 2004:143). Likewise, Şentürk points out the same schizophrenic structure noting that "the last three decades' figurative-postmodern films are running like migrants from location to location, action to action, type to type, from one narrative technique to the next, from one excess to the other. These films, with the loading of types and styles of many reality levels one top of each other, create uncertainty, coincidentality, instantness, and illegal complexity; such that they cause a concerned uneasiness and the demolition of secondary orders" (Şentürk, 2011:496). For Uçakan, the impact of the global post-modernity has displayed itself in Turkey as an original form of cinema, "the cosmopolitan cinema," and, "its only ambition and purpose consists of earning money, no artistic purpose full of ideas and aesthetics such as providing direction to society, nor an ideological responsibility exists in this purpose" (Uçakan, 2010:23).

Cinema in Turkey can surely be assessed with an analysis of its mental transformations along its own specific development in the history of Turkey. Cinema, as a field of art and communication has played an effective role, especially as far as the public adapting the Western way of life since westernization and its derivative ideologies bore vital roles on shaping the Turkish social structure. No matter westernization has carried a functionality based greatly on form rather than context, it caused social fragmentations along the Turkish society based on varying views on this unhealthy westernization phenomenon. As a result, the different solutions sought for these varying stances were projected to the screen through the eyes of the directors whose opinions have also been extremely different from each other. Due to the lack of a cinema industry in Turkey in the common sense, the economic infrastructure of Turkish Cinema has ever been left unfinished and incomplete. According to the majority of Turkish cinema producers the fact that Turkish Cinema could not undergo a natural process of industrialization has been caused by that it has ever been a cinema of the common public. The fact that most of the films has just been made to meet the need of entertainment for the cultureless and uneducated public has prevented Turkish Cinema from gaining an initiative to evolve towards becoming a well-constructed sector. Shaped for the purpose of meeting the public's need of entertainment, the artistic stance of Turkish Cinema also has accorded itself with the common tastes and demands of the public, which on the other hand, made Turkish Cinema become an area where the perception of Turkish modernization has also been projected. Nijat Özün tied the backwardness of Turkish cinema and its inability to turn into a proper cinema to two reasons: "Traditional narrative arts such as the Karagöz play, eulogy shows, encomiasts, imitators preventing the development of the language of images and the lack of picture arts traditions or drama arts to feed the cinema language" (Arslan, 2010:236). Examining Turkish films through the scope of "the concept of "structuring absences,"—the idea that any text must be judged not only by what it says, but by what it leaves out—(Gaggi, 1978:466) enlightens the essential ideological perspective in concern: "the desire to be 'modern but national' is operating ... the emotional geography of nationalism seems to have caused us to see nationalism as the hope to be saved from estrangement rather than estrangement" (Arslan, 2010:240, 355-356). Batur and his friends' brief assertion paraphrases the concern quite precisely: "the ideological dimension of Turkish cinema that does not require a great deal of effort to understand ... But in order to speak of the cynicalness of cinema, first we must dwell on what cynical consciousness is ... Cynical counsciousness is a mistaken consciousness that has absorbed being wrong, therefore, it is not easily affected by any criticism of ideology and moral judgment (1985:111-112).

For Altunışık and Tür the issue is totally different (2005): He claims that the Turkish-Islamic synthesis has become the dominant ideology in Turkey since 12 September coup, though elbowing the military custody out of Turkish cinematic art could only be realized in 2003 when "the representatives of the NSC [National Security Council] on the Supervision Board of Cinema, Video and Music were removed" (Yavuz, 2009: 272). Indeed, the coups realized in 1960, 1971, 1980 and 1997 have deeply impacted the mental and physical position of Turkish Cinema. Whereas the common view on Yeşilçam Cinema claims that "it has never owned a pre-designed intellectual foundation" (Ayça, 1996), cinema has ever been considered as an essential part of the Turkish modernization process. Concordantly, the modernizing elite have been displaying a tendency to utilize the cinematic art in the service of their social goals. Şasa notes more and asserts that "it has been the formal state ideology that orders Turkish Cinema to follow in the tracks of American and European Cinemas;" she keeps underlining that the same ideological center "prevents people get connected with their own real history and historical positions; as the social memory has ceaselessly been castrated, the collective symbols and values, and all the deep-rooted archetypes have been set back in the consciousness of our people" (Şasa, 1993:150). That is, the fact that the Turkish Cinema along 90s and 2000s includes the individualistic expressions and art forms at an increasing level towards the 'author cinema' does not mean much in the whole picture.

The Name of the Hope: The Conservative Turkish Cinema—The Efforts of Yücel Çakmaklı and His Disciples

Cündioğlu underlines the universal stance of the Muslim consciousness against the visual and visualization of objects informing that "the Muslim consciousness has always closed its eyes for listening, thinking and imagining. It has tried to grasp objects with its ears rather than its eyes. Throughout history, this religious consciousness has always felt disturbed from the sketching and description of objects, especially living beings. It did not like objects to be imparted continuity and permanency to objects visually. It has estimated a weakness to worship idols by imparting continuity and permanency to objects. It has feared the replacement of the visualizer by the visualized. This consciousness structure has perceived the presence of pictures and sculptures as an ideological threat" (2013:145). It is this assumption of threat towards the essence of belief and faith, the Turkish artists who have felt themselves somewhat conservative or pious, have had great difficulty to work on the visual arts or arts containing visualization of objects. As a by-product of this notion, "the people of this country [Turkey] did not see a color inspired by their own culture, their own religion and their own spirits in the cinema ... The cinema was foreign, there was a strange look in the films. In some films they almost saw an "enemy" look. Historical and spiritual values were mocked ... For this reason, the hearts of the nation and cinema never met, 'cinema' ... could not make peace with the culture of the people and their spiritual world" till the emergence of Yücel Çakmaklı (Uyar, 2010:335-337) (Dumanlı, 2009:28,29,45) (Enderun, 2011:13). It was him "through [whose] films, the people of this nation noticed that cinema was actually a beautiful and useful art, rather than a weapon aimed at their own spiritual lives. And they started to like the cinema ... He joined cinema with the cultural and spiritual values of the nation; he made peace between the people and cinema" (Uyar, 2010:338).

The ecole pioneered by Çakmaklı has been entitled with varying modifications along the history of Turkish Cinema such as "the White Cinema" (Hazar, 2010:221), "the Islamist Cinema, the Green Cinema, the Cinema of True-Path, Milli Cinema, the Cinema of Faith, the Cinema of Dream, the Cinema of Spirituality, and the Cinema of Purification" (Yenen, 2012:240,244). Whatever it may be called, Uçakan argues "to use a soft expression," and offers a catch-all term, "making cinema in Muslim-like manner" (Tosun, 1992:37). The clarification of Uçakan's "making cinema in Muslim-like manner" is done by himself in a precise way, indicating that "Islam does not look at art as the Molotov cocktail of the guerillas, an advertising element of capital, nor a motive that ensures that those with fat wallets get busy their own nonsense." As one of the essential disciples of Çakmaklı, he does not neglect to point out the close affiliation between Islam and art: "According to Islam, "art is a supreme task that carries the concern of making the realities of creation, researching the purpose for the creation of nature and man, the demands and wishes aimed at the eternal and permanent beauty of the creations from the enchanting beauty of the Creator in the depths of human emotion and thought" (Uçakan, 2010:158-159). The moderate interpretation of this ecole is naturally considered as a positive development, as Özdemir comments that the films produced in Turkey in 2000s signify "an approach where a concept of religion as a part of life is emphasized ... rather than an understanding of religion as a basis of life" (2011:28). Şasa, one of the eminent Turkish cinema thinkers and practitioners, points out the most critical problematic of Turkish Cinema has been lying under the fact that

> the foundation of cinema technique is social culture. Every society or every unit of civilization has to establish and develop the main core of the cinema technique—its cinematography—in accordance with the function of its own social culture. This is especially the case in countries such as ours possessing a very unique foundation of civilization and should be this way. A three layer process should be considered. Social culture takes place at the lowest layer, on top of it a cinema language established in accordance with the function of that culture—cinema technique can gain a real function only when it is used to build a live language suited to the living cultural foundation—on top of that an artistic superstructure, the cinematic art of that society. (2003:34).

As the traditional Turkish Cinema has ever acted in contrast to these dramatic determinations, it has been vastly criticized being "broken off from the social structure of Turkish society" (Turan, 2007:90). Fictionalizing merely narrative structures conforming to the modernization policies of governments and Kemalist nationalism, this structure has ever been the mere cinematic representative of the introverted formative modernization policies since the beginning days of the Republic. Battal's notes on the tragedy and absurdity of this position point out the vital problematic:

> The ideological and political quality of Turkish cinema has been a spontaneous projection of the existing ruling ideology. The relation of cinema with the government has been created with censorship and its pressure in order to preserve this existing structure recreated in cinema. It is not possible for the traditional Turkish cinema to have a problem with the political authority since this cinema is already in the position of being a voluntary bearer of the ideology of the political power. A content that is the mixture of an artificial culture as a result of imitating the west and the traditional culture was produced and made extensive in traditional Turkish cinema. An operation channeled within the chain of surprising multitude and complexity all the way from the most degenerate imitations of the west to the most pompous eastern melodramas or a showing or warning based on personal efforts demonstrates

> the irrationality in this area and the confusion caused by internal and external conditions. Not based on rational grounds, the lack of meaning in dialogues of Yesilçam films is very suited to the principle 'having to say everything to the end in order to arrive at expressions that say nothing'. Stories and narration techniques are lacking depth and credibility since they are produced through imitations. (2006:113-114).

Noticed or unnoticed by the vast majority, the art of cinema in Turkey has always been—directly or indirectly—controlled and framed by the formal authorities. And the result, regret to declare, has been not too much different from the failure that Scognamillo warns about: "when cinema takes place next to an ideology or a political tendency, it becomes a 'message' carrier within its "show/entertainment' qualities—in fact either exceeding or forgetting those qualities. When it became a 'state cinema' bound to a government it followed the same path, it renounced all free and unbiased expressions, compromised, giving up its real creativity and creators, quieted them and became non-identifiable" (1998:183). Although a sharply outlined ideology could not simply be described for Turkish Cinema, modernization policies with many ways have transcended the spirit of filmatic creation. Neither a specific Turkish cinema language, nor a form or stance, nor a philosophy has emerged so far due to the blinkers of Kemalist nationalism, westernism, and positivism indoctrinated specifically upon the Turkish cinematic circles, the entire Turkish society in general.

Whereas the formal objective of Turkey has been determined by state authorities as 'westernization at all costs' for almost two hundred years, the core truth does not change: the thought universe of Turkey has ever leaned on the East. In this regard, no matter the art and industry of cinema is a western phenomenon, Turkish Cinema is expected to correspond to a specific sphere where the western cinema merges with the eastern universe of thought. As Altan offers "when Turkish cinema makes peace with its own cultural treasure that has fed and watered this land for centuries without breaking off from its own public and values, it will find its own local identity and will tell people of the world what they have not yet heard to date" (Altan,

2010:74). That is, "Turkish Cinema should save itself from the disease of looking at its own history with an ideological trepidation or even negatively and it should have a clearer point of view towards its past" (Acar, 2010:50). Uçakan diagnoses the ages-old illness: "Turkey is facing a serious identity frustration today. Yeşilcam [Turkish Cinema] has been experiencing the pains of this crisis and the clogging brought about by these pains" (Uçakan, 2007:112). It shall surely be fruitful to confront the aesthetic, technological, and ideological assumptions in existing "deeply nationalist and secular" Turkish cinema approaches with the real social values of the Turkish society. Only with this strategy, it may be possible to suggest by extension some more specificity and substance to the more general issues vexing current Turkish Cinema. To attain a cinema purified from all kinds of crisis, the identity crisis at top, the "more" democracy is strongly required that is at peace with the past, present and future of Turkish society.

References

Abbott, Paul. (1979) "Authority," *Screen*, 20 (2), pp. 11-64.

Abisel, Nilgün. (1994) *Türk Sineması Üzerine Yazılar,* İstanbul: İmge Kitabevi.

Abisel, Nilgün. (1997) "Bir Dunya Nasıl Kurulur? Popüler Türk Filmlerinde Anlatı Yapısı Üzerine," *Sinema Yazıları,* Seçil Büker (drl), Ankara: Doruk Yayımcılık.

Abisel, Nilgün. (2005) *Türk Sineması Üzerine Yazılar*, 2. Basım, Ankara: Phoenix Yayınları.

Acar, Bedir. (2010) "Türk Sinemasında Zihniyet Açılımına İhtiyaç Var," *Türk Sinemasında Yerli Arayışlar*, ed. Abdurrahman Şen, Ankara: Kültür ve Turizm Bakanlığı.

Adıvar, Abdulhak A. (1947) "Islamic and Western Thought in Turkey," *Middle East Journal*, 1 (3), pp. 270-280.

Adorno, Theodor and Max Horkheimer. (1972) *Dialectic of Enlightenment*, trans. John Cumming, New York:Herder&Herder.

Adorno, Theodor W and Thomas Y. Levin. (1981-82) "Transparencies on Film, New German Critique," *Special Double Issue on New German Cinema*, 24 (25), pp. 199-205.

Aguiar, Marian. (2007) "Nâzim Hikmet's Modernism of Development," *Journal of Modern Literature*, 30 (4), pp. 105-121.

Ahmad, Faroz. (1993) *The Making of Modern Turkey*, London: Routledge.

Ahmad, Feroz. (1988) "Islamic Reassertion in Turkey," *Third World Quarterly*, 10 (2), pp. 750-769.

Aitken, Ian. (2009) "What is There Really in the World? Forms of Theory, Evidence and Truth in Fahrenheit 9/11: A Philosophical and Intuitionist Realist Approach," *Film Theory and Contemporary Hollywood Movies*, ed. Warren Buckland, N.York&London:Routledge.

Aitken, Ian. (1998) "Distraction and Redemption: Kracauer, Surrealism and Phenomenology," *Screen*, 39 (2), pp. 124-140.

Aksoy, Bülent. (1989) "Is the Question of the 'Origin of Turkish Music' Not Redundant?" Turkish Music Quarterly, 2 (4), pp. 1-7.

Allen, Richard. (1987) "Critical Theory and The paradox of Modernist Discourse," *Screen*, 28 (2), pp. 69-86.

Allen, Richard. (1993) "Representation, Illusion, and the Cinema," *Cinema Journal*, 32 (2), pp. 21-48.

Altan, Ömer (2010)."Sinemamizin Geleceğinde Dil ve Üslup Oluşturmanın Önemi," *Türk Sinemasında Yerli Arayışlar*, ed. Abdurrahman Şen, Ankara: Kültür ve Turizm Bakanlığı.

Althusser, L. (1970) *For Marx*, New York: Vintage Books.

Althusser, L. (1971) *Lenin and Philosophy*, London: New Left Books.

Altuğ, Taylan. (1973) "Aydınlar ve Türk Sinemasının Sorunları," *Yedinci Sanat*, 10, pp. 48-69.

Altunışık, M.Benli and Özlem Tür. (2005) *Turkey: Challenges of Continuity and Change*, London&N.York: Routledge.

Andrew, Dudley. (2000) "The 'Three Ages' of Cinema Studies and the Age to Come," *PMLA*, 115 (3), pp. 341-351.

Anonymous. (1973) "MTTB Sinema Kulübü Milli Sinema Açık Oturum," *MTBB Sinema Kulübü Yayınları:1, Açık Oturum Dizisi:1*, İstanbul: Güryay Matbaacılık.

Armağan, Mustafa. (1999) "Alternatif Modernliğe ve Modernliğimize Dair," *Doğu-Batı*, 8, pp. 83-93.

Aronowitz, Stanley. (1979) "Film: The Art Form of Late Capitalism," *Social Text*, 1, pp. 110-129.

Arslan, Savaş. (1997) "Popüler Yeşilçam Filmlerinin Eleştirilmesinde Bir Sanat Sineması Söyleminin Oluşumu," *25. Kare*, 20, pp. 45-53.

Arslan, T. Umut. (2010) *Mazi Kabrinin Hortlakları*, Istanbul: Metis Yayınları.

Ayça, Engin. (2003) "Yeşilçam Sonrası," *Antrakt*, 75–76, p. 18-32.

Ayça, Engin (1996). "Yeşilçama Bakış," ed. Süleyman Murat Dinçer, *Türk Sineması Üstüne Düşünceler*, Ankara: Doruk Yayınları.

Aydın, Mukadder Ç. (1997) "1960'lar Türkiye'sinde Sinemadaki Akımlar," *25. Kare*, 21, pp. 12-20.

Balides, Constance. (1993) "Scenarios of Exposure in the Practice of Everyday Life: Women in the Cinema of Attractions," *Screen*, 34 (1), pp. 19-37.

Balides, Constance. (2000) "Jurassic Post-Fordism: Tall Tales of Economics in the Theme Park," *Screen*, 41 (2), pp. 139-160.

Balkin, J.M. (1998) *Cultural Software*, New Haven and London: Yale University Press.

Barthes, Roland. (1970) *Mythologies*, 2nd ed., Paris: Seuil.

Battal, Sadık. (2006) *Asıl Film Şimdi Başlıyor*, Ankara: Vadi Yayınları.

Batur Enis, Onat Kutlar, Metin Erksan. (1985) *Ve Sinema*, Istanbul: Hilal Yayınları.

Baudry, Jean-Louis and Alan Williams. (1974) "Ideological Effects of the Basic Cinematographic Apparatus," *Film Quarterly*, 28 (2), pp. 39-47.

Bayar, Ali H. (1996) "The Developmental State and Economic Policy in Turkey," *Third World Quarterly*, 17 (4), pp. 773-785.

Bazin, Andre. (2005) *What is Cinema II?*, Berkeley & Los Angeles: University of California Press.

Behçetogulları, Pembe. (2002) Türkiye'de Ulusal Sinema ve Ulusal Sinema Söylemi. Ankara Üniversitesi, Sosyal Bilimler Enstitüsü, Basılmamış Doktora Tezi, Ankara.

Beller, Jonathan L. (1995) "The Spectatorship of the Proletariat," *Boundary 2*, 22 (3) pp. 171-228.

Belge, Murat. (1983) "Türkiye'de Günlük Hayat," *Cumhuriyet Dönemi Türkiye Ansiklopedisi*, C. 3, İstanbul: İletişim Yayınları.

Ben-Ghiat, Ruth. (1996) "Envisioning Modernity: Desire and Discipline in the Italian Fascist Film," *Critical Inquiry*, 23 (1), pp. 109-144.

Bordwell, David. (1988) "Adventures in The Highlands of Theory," 20 (1), pp. 72-07.

Bostan, Erman and Zahit Atam. (2006) "Melodramdan Yansıyan 12 Eylül Üzerine Provakatif Düşünceler," *Yeni İnsan Yeni Sinema*, 18-19.

Bozdoğan, Sibel and Reşat Kasaba (1997). "Introduction," eds. Sibel Bozdoğan and Reşat Kasaba, *Rethinking Modernity and National Identity in Turkey*, Seattle and London: University of Washington Press.

Brown, Bill. (1998) "Identity Culture," American *Literary History*, 10 (1), pp. 164-184.

Buckingham, David. (1986) "Against Demystification: A Response to Teaching the Media," *Screen*, 27 (5), pp. 80-95.

Buckland, Warren (ed). (2009) *Film Theory and Contemporary Hollywood Movies*, N.York & London: Routledge.

Buckland, Warren. (1989) "Critique of Poor Reason," *Screen*, 30 (4), pp. 80-103.

Burch, Noël. (1979) "Film's Institutional Mode of Representation and the Soviet Response," 11, pp. 77-96.

Büker, Seçil. (2002) "The Film Does Not End with an Ecstatic Kiss," eds. Deniz Kandiyoti and Ayşe Saktanber, *Fragments of Culture*, London: I.B.Tauris & Co. Ltd.

Büker, Seçil and Canan Uluyağcı. (1993) *Yeşilçam'da Bir Sultan*, İstanbul: AFA Yayıncılık.

Cantor, Paul A. (2006) "Film Noir and the Frankfurt School: America as Wasteland in Edgar Ulmer's Detour," ed. Mark T.Conard, *The Philosophy of Film Noir*, Kentucky: The University Press of Kentucky.

Carroll, Noël. (1990) "The Image of Women in Film: A Defense of a Paradigm," *The Journal of Aesthetics and Art Criticism*, 48 (4), pp. 349-360.

Carroll, Noël. (1985) "The Power of Movies," *Daedalus*, 114 (4), pp. 79-103.

Carroll, Noel. (1988) *Mystifying Movies: Fads and Fallacies in Contemporary Film Theory*, New York: Columbia UP.

Cegarra, Michel. (1973) "Cinema and Semiology," *Screen*, 14 (1-2), pp. 129-188.

Chanan, Michael. (1997) "The Changing Geography of Third Cinema," *Screen*, 38 (4), pp. 372-388.

Chapman, James. (2003) *Cinemas of the World*, London: Reaktion Books.

Christian, Re'ka. (2011) "The Male Gaze," ed. Philip C. Dimare, *Movies in American History-An Encyclopedia*, 1, Santa Barbara: ABC Clio.

Cizre, Ümit. (2005) "12 Eylül'ün 'Anti' Gündeminde Toplum," *Toplumsal Tarih*, 141, pp. 24-28.

Collins, James. (1987) "Postmodernism and Cultural Practice: Redifining The Parameters," *Screen*, 28 (2), pp. 11-27.

Comolli, Jean-Luc and Paul Narboni. (1971) "Cinema-Ideology-Criticism," *Screen*, 12 (1), pp. 27-38.

Connell, Ian. (1978) "Ideology/Discourse/Institution," *Screen*, 19 (3), .pp. 129-134.

Cooper, Mark Garrett. (1998) "Love, Danger, and the Professional Ideology of Hollywood Cinema," *Cultural Critique*, 39, pp. 85-117.

Cooper, Mark Garrett. (2002) "Narrative Spaces," *Screen*, 43 (2), pp. 139.157.

Coş, Nezih. (1987) "Örgütlenme Gereği," *Ve Sinema*, 4, İstanbul: Hil Yayınları.

Coward, Rosalind. (1977) "Class, Culture and the Social Formation," *Screen*, 18 (1), pp. 75-106.

Culler, Jonathan. (1973) "Structure of Ideology and Ideology of Structure," *New Literary History*, 4 (3), pp. 471-482.

Cündioğlu, Dücane. (2005) *Meşrutiyetten Cumhuriyete Din ve Siyaset*, Istanbul: Kaknüs Yayınları.

Cündioğlu, Dücane. (2013) *Sanat ve Felsefe*, İstanbul: Kapı Yayınları.

Çağaptay, Soner. (2006) *Islam, Secularism, and Nationalism in Modern Turkey*, London&N.York: Routledge.

Çokyiğit, Coşkun. (2010) "Milli sinema mi, Milli Estetik mi?," ed. Abdurrahman Şen, *Türk Sinemasında Yerli Arayışlar*, Ankara: Kültür ve Turizm Bakanlığı.

Daldal, Aslı. (2003) "Toplumsal Gerçekliğe Doğru: 1950'lerin Sinema Ortamı," *Yeni Film*, 1, s.43–44.

Daldal, Aslı. (2005) *1960 Darbesi ve Türk Sinemasında Toplumsal Gerçekçilik*, İstanbul: Homer Kitapevi.

Darke, Chris. (1993) "Rupture, Continuity and Diversification: Cahiers du Cinema in the 1980s," *Screen*, 34 (4), pp. 362-379.

Demir, A. İshak. (2004) *Cumhuriyet Dönemi Aydınlarının İslam'a Bakışı*, Istanbul: Ensar Neşriyat.

Diriklik, Salih. *(1995) Fleşbek, Cilt 1,* İstanbul: Kendi Yayını.

Dittmar, Linda. (1995) "All That Hollywood Allows: Film and the Working Class," *The Radical Teacher*, 46, pp. 38-45.

Doğan, Ayşe Ş. (2010) "Dünya Penceresinden Türk Sineması," *Türk Sinemasında Yerli Arayışlar*, ed. Abdurrahman Şen. Ankara: Kültür ve Turizm Bakanlığı.

Dorsay, Atilla. (2003) *Sinema ve Çağımız*, İstanbul: Remzi Kitabevi.

Dorsay, Atilla (1998). "Cumhuriyetimizin Bir Diğer Kurumu Sinemamıza Bir Bakış Denemesi," *Cumhuriyet IV*, pp. 3163-3168. Dorsay, Atilla. (1989) *Sinemamızın Umut Yılları: 1970/80 Arası Türk Sinemasına Bakışlar*, İstanbul: İnkılap Kitabevi.

Dorsay, Atilla. (1984) *Sinema ve Çağımız–1*, İstanbul: Hil Yayınları.

Dorsay, Atilla. (1985) *Sinemayı Sanat Yapanlar*, Istanbul: Varlık Yayınları.

Downing, David B. and Susan Bazargan. (1991) *Image and Ideology in Modern/Postmodern Discourse.*, N.York: State University of New York Press.

Dönmez-Colin, Gönül. (2004) *Women, İslam and Cinema*, London: Reaktion Books.

Dumanlı, Ekrem. (2009) *Sinemaya Farklı Yerden Bakma,* İstanbul: Zaman Kitap.

Durant, Alan. (2000) "What future for interpretive work in Film and Media Studies?," *Screen*, 41(1), pp. 7-17.

Dworkin, Martin S. (1977) "Criticism and Ideology: A Note on Cinema," *Journal of Aesthetic Education*, 11(4), pp. 93-101.

Eagleton, Terry. (1976) *Marxism and Literary Criticism*, Berkeley: University of California Press.

Eagleton, Terry. (1978) *Criticism and Ideology,* London: Verso.

Eagleton, Terry. (1991) *Ideology: An Introduction*, London: Verso.

Eaton, Mick. (1976) "Anthropology and Film," *Screen*, 17 (3), pp. 113-118.

Elsaesser, Thomas. (1975) "The Pathos of Failure: American Films in the 70s—Notes on the Unmotivated Hero," Monogram, 6, pp. 13-19.

Elsaesser, Thomas. (2005) *European Cinema-Face to Face with Hollywood*, Amsterdam: Amsterdam University Press.

Enderun, M. Akif. (2011) *Beyaz Perdenin Din Algısı*, Izmir: Işık Yayınları.

Erdemir, Tanyeri Tuğba. (2006) "Archaeology as a Source of National Pride in the Early Years of the Turkish Republic," *Journal of Field Archaeology*, 31 (4), pp. 381-393.

Erdoğan, Nezih. (2001) "Üç Seyirci: Popüler Eğlence Biçimlerinin Alımlanması Üzerine Notlar," *Doğu-Batı*, 15, pp. 109-120.

Erdoğan, Nezih. (1998) "Narratives of Resistance: National Identity and Ambivalence in the Turkish Melodrama between 1965 and 1975," *Screen*, 39 (3), pp. 259-271.

Esen, Şükran. (2000) *80'ler Türkiyesi'nde Sinema*, Istanbul: Beta Yayıncılık.

Evren, Burçak. (2010) "Türk Sinemasında Değişim-Dönüşüm Dönemeci," *Türk Sinemasında Yerli Arayışlar*, ed. Abdurrahman Şen, Ankara: Kültür ve Turizm Bakanlığı.

Evren, Burçak. (1994) "Devlet ve Sanat," Milliyet, 10 Aralık 1994.

Feldman, Walter. (1990) "Cultural Authority and Authenticity in the Turkish Repertoire," *Asian Music*, 22 (1), pp. 73-111.

Feldmann, Martha J. (1995) "Totalitarianism without Pain: Teaching Communism and Fascism with Film," *The History Teacher*, Vol. 29 (1), pp. 51-61.

Fell, John. (1981) "Theory," *Film Quarterly*, 34 (4), pp. 59-60.

Ferenz, Volker. (2009) "Mementos of Contemporary American Cinema: Identifying and Responding to the Unreliable Narrator in the Movie Theater," ed. Warren Buckland, *Film Theory and Contemporary Hollywood Movies*, N. York & London: Routledge.

Fletcher, John. (1988) "Melodrama: An Introduction," *Screen*, 29 (3), pp. 2-12.

Foucault, Michel. (1980) "Truth and Power," *Power/Knowledge: Selected Interviews and Other Writings 1972–1977*, trans. C. Gordon, L. Marshall, J. Mepham and K. Soper, New York: Pantheon Books.

reeden, Michael. (2003) *Ideology: A Very Short Introduction*, Cornwall: Oxford.

Frey, Mattias. (2010) "Cultural Problems of Classical Film Theory: Béla Balázs, 'Universal Language' and the Birth of National Cinema," *Screen*, 51(4), pp. 324-340.

Friedman, R. M. (1984) "Exorcising the Past: Jewish Figures in Contemporary Films," *Journal of Contemporary History*, 19 (3), pp. 511-527.

Gaggi, Silvio. (1978) "Semiology, Marxism, and the Movies," *The Journal of Aesthetics and Art Criticism*, 36 (4), pp. 461-469.

Gallie, W. B. and Cyril Barrett. (1972) "Art and Politics," *Proceedings of the Aristotelian Society*, Supplementary Volumes, 46, pp. 103-138.

Gidal, Peter. (1979) "The Anti-Narrative," *Screen*, 20 (2), pp. 73-93.

Gidal, Peter. (1984) "Against Sexual Representation In Film," *Screen*, 25 (6), pp. 24-30.

Gottdiener, M. (1993) "Ideology, Foundationalism, and Sociological Theory," *The Sociological Quarterly*, 34 (4), pp. 653-671.

Gökmen, Salih. (1973a) *Milli Sinema Açık Oturumu Ardından*, İstanbul:Hisar Yayınları.

Gökmen, Salih. (1973b) *Bugünkü Türk Sineması*, İstanbul:Fetih Yayınevi.

Göle, Nilüfer. (1997a) "Secularism and Islamism in Turkey: The Making of Elites and Counter-Elites," *Middle East Journal*, 51 (1), pp. 46-58.

Göle, Nilüfer. (1997b) *Modern Mahrem*, İstanbul: Metis Yayınları.

Göle, Nilüfer. (2000) *Melez Desenler*, İstanbul: Metis Yayınları.

Green, Philip. (1993) "Ideology and Ambiguity in Cinema," *The Massachusetts Review*, Vol. 34 (1), pp. 102-126.

Greene, Naomi. (1974) "Esthetics and Politics in Cinematic Language," *Sub-Stance*, 3 (9), pp. 137-143.

Grieveson, Lee. (2009) "On Governmentality and Screens," *Screen*, 50 (1), pp. 180-187.

Guzzetti, Alfred. (1973) "Christian Metz and the Semiology of the Cinema," *Journal of Modern Literature*, 3 (2), pp. 292-308.

Güçhan, Gülseren. (1992) *Toplumsal Değişme Ve Türk Sineması*, Ankara: İmge Yayınları.

Güneş, İsmail. (2010) "Çağın Abide Sanatı: Sinema," ed. Abdurrahman Şen, *Türk Sinemasında Yerli Arayışlar*, Ankara: Kültür ve Turizm Bakanlığı.

Güney, Yılmaz. (2000) *Siyasal Yazılar*, İstanbul: Güney Yayınları.

Güney, Yılmaz. (2003) *İnsan, Militan ve Sanatçı Yılmaz Güney*, İstanbul: Güney Filmcilik.

Güven, A. Murat. (2009) "Türk Sineması'nın Din ve Dindarlikla 95 Yıllık İmtihanı," *Din ve Hayat Dergisi*, 3, pp. 105-106.

Güven, Yusuf. (2004) "Türk Sinemasının Son Dönemi," *Yeni Film*, 7, pp. 22-34.

Halachmi, Joseph. (1998) "Abraham Neufeld and the Beginnings of the Zionist Film," *Film History*, 10 (1), pp. 90-97.

Hansen, Miriam. (1992) "Mass Culture as Hieroglyphic Writing: Adorno, Derrida, Kracauer," *New German Critique*, 56, pp. 43-73.

Hansen, Miriam. (1993) "Early Cinema, Late Vinema: Permutations of the Public Sphere," *Screen*, 34 (3), pp. 197-210.

Harpole, Charles H. (1980) "Ideological and Technological Determinism in Deep-Space Cinema Images: Issues in Ideology, Technological History, and Aesthetics," *Film Quarterly*, 33 (3), pp. 11-22.

Hawkes, David. (2003) *Ideology*, 2nd ed., London and N.York: Routledge.

Hayward, Susan. (2000) *Cinema Studies: The Key Concepts*, 2nd ed., London&N. York: Routledge.

Hazar, Nedim. (2010) "Türk Sinemasında Yerli Arayışların Kısa Tarihçesi," ed. Abdurrahman Şen, *Türk Sinemasında Yerli Arayışlar*, Ankara: Kültür ve Turizm Bakanlığı.

Hazar, Nedim. (2004) "İdeolojik Sanat Geri Dönüyor," *Zaman Gazetesi*, 25.02.2004.

Henderson, Brian. (1975) "Metz: Essais I and Film Theory," *Film Quarterly*, 28 (3), pp. 18-33.

Heper, Metin. (1991) "The State, Religion and Pluralism: The Turkish Case in Comparative Perspective," *British Journal of Middle Eastern Studies*, 18 (1), pp. 38-51.

Hikmet, Nazım, Soupault, Philippe. (1964) *Anthologie Poetique*, Paris: Les Editeurs Francais Reunis.

Hillier, Jim. (1986) *Cahiers De Cinema 1960-1968: New Wave, New Cinema, Reevaluating Hollywood*, Cambridge: Harvard University Press.

Howard, Harry N. (1939) "Turkey," *The Phi Delta Kappan*, 22 (3), pp. 79-82, 86.

Hudson, Dale and Patricia R. Zimmermann. (2009) "Clinephilia, Technophilia and Collaborative Remix Zones," *Screen*, 50 (1), pp. 135-146.

Hunt, Leon and Leung Wing-Fai (ed). (2008) *East Asian Cinemas*, London&N. York: I.B.Tauris.

İrem, Nazım. (2002) "Turkish Conservative Modernism: Birth of a Nationalist Quest for Cultural Renewal," *International Journal of Middle East Studies*, 34 (1), pp. 87-112.

Jacobs, Lewis. (1967) "World War II and the American Film," *Cinema Journal*, 7, pp. 1-21.

Jess-Cooke, Carolyn. (2009) *Film Sequels*, Edinburgh: Edinburgh University Press.

Johnson, William C. Jr. (1979) "Literature, Film, and the Evolution of Consciousness," *The Journal of Aesthetics and Art Criticism*, 38 (1), pp. 29-38.

Jones-Thomson, Katherine. (2008) *Aesthetics and Film*, London&N.York: Continuum.

Kadıoğlu, Ayşe. (1996) "The Paradox of Turkish Nationalism and the Construction of Official Identity," *Middle Eastern Studies*, Vol. 32 (2), pp. 177-193.

Kahraman, B.Hasan. (2010) "Sinema Kavgasıyla Ölmek," ed. Abdurrahman Şen, *Türk Sinemasında Yerli Arayışlar*, Ankara: Kültür ve Turizm Bakanlığı.

Kalaycıoğlu, Ersin. (1980) "Why Legislatures Persist in Developing Countries: The Case of Turkey," *Legislative Studies Quarterly*, 5(1), pp. 123-140.

Kaplan, Sam. (2002) "Din-u Devlet All over Again? The Politics of Military Secularism and Religious Militarism inTurkey following the 1980 Coup." *International Journal of Middle East Studies*, 34 (1), pp. 113-127.

Karaömerlioğlu, M. Asım. (1998) "The People's Houses and the Cult of the Peasant in Turkey," *Middle Eastern Studies*, 34 (4), pp. 67-91.

Karpat, Kemal H. (1975) "The Memoirs of N. Batzaria: The Young Turks and Nationalism," *International Journal of Middle East Studies*, 6 (3), pp. 276-299.

Karpat, Kemal H. (1966) "The Turkish Left," *Journal of Contemporary History*, 1 (2), pp. 169-186.

Karpat, Kemal H. (1963) "The People's Houses in Turkey: Establishment and Growth," *Middle East Journal*, 17 (1/2), pp. 55-67.

Karpat, Kemal H. (2004) "The Status of Ideology in Turkey Today," *East-West*, 30, p. 25-26.

Karpat, Kemal H. (2011) *Türk Siyasi Tarihi: Siyasal Sistemin Evrimi*, Istanbul: Timaş Yayınları.

Kavanagh, Thomas M. (1979) "The Middle Voice of Film Narration," *Diacritics*, 9 (3), pp. 54-61.

Kaya, İbrahim. (2004) *Social Theory and Later Modernities: The Turkish Experience*, Liverpool: Liverpool University Press.

Kayalı, Kurtuluş. (2006) *Yönetmenler Çerçevesinde Türk Sineması*, Ankara: Deniz Yayınları.

Kedourie, Elie. (1968) "The End of the Ottoman Empire," *Journal of Contemporary History*, 3 (4), pp. 19-28.

Kerslake, Celia, Kerem Öktem, Philip Robins (ed). (2010) *Turkey's Engagement with Modernity*, N.York: Palgrave Macmillan.

Kılınç, Aygül. (2005) *Atatürk Dönemi Kültür Politikasının Türk Toplumsal Yaşamına Etkileri ve Katkıları*, Basılmamış Y.Lisans Tezi, Malatya: İnönü Üniversitesi Ssosyal Bilimler Enstitüsü.

Kiernan, Maureen. (1990) "Making Films Politically: Marxism in Eisenstein and Godard," *Alif Journal of Comparative Poetics*, 10, pp. 93-113.

Kinloch, C. Graham and Raj P.Mohan (ed). *Ideology and The Social Sciences*, Westport: Greenwood Press.

Klinger, Barbara. (1984) "Cinema/Ideology/Criticism' Revisited: The Progressive Text," *Screen*, 25 (1), pp. 30-44.

Klinger, Barbara. (1997) "Film History Terminable and Interminable," *Screen*, 38 (2), pp. 107-128.

Knight, Deborah. (1993) "Reconsidering Film Theory and Method," *New Literary History*, 24 (2), pp. 321-338.

Knight, Deborah. (1997) "Back to Basics: Film/Theory/Aesthetics," *Journal of Aesthetic Education*, 31 (2), pp. 37-44.

Koçer, Suat. (2010) "Yoksulluk ve Yoksunluk Ekseninde: Zeki Ökten Sineması," ed. Abdurrahman Şen, *Türk Sinemasında Yerli Arayışlar*, Ankara: Kültür ve Turizm Bakanlığı.

Kongar, Emre. (1999) *Toplumsal Değişme Kuramları ve Türkiye Gerçeği*, 7.Basım, İstanbul: Bilgi Yayınevi.

Kuhn, Annette. (1977) "Film Culture: Camera Obscura," *Screen*, 18 (2), pp. 123-128.

Kuntzel, Thierry. (1973) "The Treatment of Ideology in the Textual Analysis of Film," *Screen*, 14 (3), pp. 44-54.

Kuru, T. Ahmet. (2011) *Pasif ve Dışlayıcı Laiklik: ABD, Fransa ve Türkiye*, Istanbul: İstanbul Bilgi Üniversitesi Yayınları.

Kushner, David. (1997) "Self-Perception and Identity in Contemporary Turkey," *Journal of Contemporary History*, 32 (2), pp. 219-233.

Lewis, Bernard. The Ottoman Empire and Its Aftermath Journal of Contemporary History, Vol. 15, No. 1, Imperial Hangovers (Jan., 1980), pp. 27-36.

Lovell, Terry. (1973) "Cultural Studies," *Screen*, 14 (3), pp. 115-122.

Lüleci, Yalçın. (2009) *Türk Sineması ve Din*, İstanbul: Es Yayınları.

MacBean, James Roy. (1972) "Godard and the Dziga Vertov Group: Film and Dialectics," *Film Quarterly*, 26 (1), pp. 30-44.

MacCabe, Colin. (1976) "Theory and Film: Principles of Realism and Pleasure," *Screen*, 17 (3), pp. 7-28.

MacDonald, Agnes Vashegyi. (2009) "The "Lukács Effect" in Twentieth-Century Hungarian Literature and Film," *Rocky Mountain Review*, 63 (1), pp. 26-42.

Magnarella, Paul J. (1970) "From Villager to Townsman in Turkey," *Middle East Journal*, 24 (2), pp. 229-240.

Makal, Oğuz. (2003) *Beyazperde ve Sahnede Nazım Hikmet*, Istanbul: YGS Yayınları.

Maktav, H. (2004) *Kuran'dan Kurama İslami Sinema*. Modern Türkiye'de Siyasi Düşünce. İslamcılık, c,VI, Istanbul: Iletişim Yayınları.

Maktav, H. (2000) "Türk Sinemasında 68'liler ve 12 Mart," *Birikim*, 132, pp. 86-92.

Maktav, Hilmi. (2010) "Sinema ya da İlahi Aşk: İslami Sinemada Tasavvufi Yolculuklar," *Sinecine: Sinema Araştırmaları Dergisi*, 1(2), pp. 31-55.

Malesevic, Sinisa. (2006) *Identity as Ideology*, N.York: Palgrave McMillan.

Maltby, Richard. (1984) "Film Noir": The Politics of the Maladjusted," *Journal of American Studies*, 18 (1), pp. 49-71.

Mango, Andrew. (1968) "Turkey in the Middle East," *Journal of Contemporary History*, 3 (3), pp. 225-236.

Maraşlı, G. Nezaket. (2010) "Türk Sinemasinda Ulusal ve Milli Sinemanin Yeri," ed. Abdurrahman Şen, *Türk Sinemasında Yerli Arayışlar*, Ankara: Kültür ve Turizm Bakanlığı.

Mardin, Serif A. (1971) "Ideology and Religion in the Turkish Revolution," *International Journal of Middle East Studies*, 2 (3), pp. 197-211.

Martin, Adrian. (2000) "The Offended Critic: The Art of Film Reviewing and Social Commentary," *Australian Quarterly*, 72 (2), pp. 10-16.

May, John R. (2001) "Toward a Christian Personalist Theory of Film," *Religion & Literature*, 33 (3), pp. 53-70.

Mazıcı, Nurşen. (2011) *Tek Parti Dönemi*, Istanbul: Pozitif Yayınları.

McConnell, Frank D. (1972) "Film and Writing: The Political Dimension," *The Massachusetts Review*, 13 (4), pp. 543-562.

McGowan, Todd. (2007) *The Real Gaze—Film Theory after Lacan*, New York: State University of New York Press.

Menekşe, Ömer. (2005) "Türk Sinemasında Din ve Din Adamı İmaji," *II. Uluslararası Dini Yayınlar Kongresi*, Ankara:Diyanet Işleri Başkanlığı Yayınları.

Metz, Christian and Alfred Guzzetti. (1976) "The Fiction Film and Its Spectator: A Metapsychological Study," *New Literary History*, 8 (1), pp. 75-105.

Michelson, Annette. (1976) "Reading Eisenstein Reading "Capital," *October*, 2, pp. 26-38.

Mitchell, Stanley. (1971) "Marinetti and Mayakovsky: Futurism, Fascism, Communism," *Screen*, 12 (4), pp. 152-161.

Mitchell, W. J. Thomas. (1987) *Iconology: Image, Text, Ideology*, Chicago: The University of Chicago Press.

Miyasoğlu, Mustafa. (2010) "Sinemada Yerli Tavırlar ve Yeni Yüzler," ed. Abdurrahman Şen, *Türk Sinemasında Yerli Arayışlar*, Ankara: Kültür ve Turizm Bakanlığı.

Mukerji, Chandra and Michael Schudson. (1986) "Popular Culture," *Annual Review of Sociology*, 12, pp. 47-66.

Naremore, James. (1990) "Authorship and the Cultural Politics of Film Criticism," *Film Quarterly*, 44 (1), pp. 14-23.

Neale, Steve. (1977) "Propaganda," *Screen*, 18 (3), pp. 9-40.

Neale, Steve. (1990) "Questions of Genre," *Screen*, 31 (1), pp. 45-66.

Neyzi, Leyla. (2001) "Object or Subject: The Paradox of "Youth" in Turkey," *International Journal of Middle East Studies*, 33 (3), pp. 411-432.

Nowell-Smith, G. (2003) "Sosyalizm, Faşizm ve Demokrasi," ed.G.Nowell-Smith, *Dünya Sinema Tarihi*, pp. 385-395, İstanbul:Kabalcı Yayınları.

O'Flinn, Paul. (1999) "Leaving the West and Entering the East': Refiğuring the Alien from Stoker to Coppola," (eds) Deborah Cartmell, I.Q. Hunter, Heidi Kaye and Imelda Whelehan, *Alien Identities*, London&Sterling: Pluto Press.

Oktay, Ahmet. (2002) *Türkiye'de Popüler Kültür*, 4. Basım, İstanbul: Everest Yayınları.

Oktay, Ahmet. (1987) *Toplumsal Değişme ve Basın*, İstanbul: Bilim Felsefe ve Sanat Yayınları.

Oktay, Ahmet. (2000) *Toplumcu Gerçekçiliğin Kaynakları*, İstanbul: Akyüz Kitapevi.

O'Shea, Alan and Bill Schwarz. (1987) "Reconsidering Popular Culture," *Screen*, 28 (3), pp. 104-109.

Oskay, Ünsal. (1996) "Sinemanın Yüzüncü Yılında Türk Sinemasında Entelektüellik Tartısmalar," ed. Murat Dinçer, *Türk Sineması Üzerine Düşünceler*, Istanbul: Doruk Yayınları.

Öndin, Nilüfer. (2003) *Cumhuriyetin Kültür Politikası ve Sanat 1923-1950*, İstanbul: İnsancıl Yayınları.

Özdemir, Hikmet. (1995) *Çağdaş Türkiye Tarihi*, Cilt 4, İstanbul: Cem Yayınevi.

Özdemir, Özlem. (2011) "Yeni Dönem İslami Sinema ve Modernlik-Geleneksellik Sınırında Üslup Arayışı," *Sine Cine: Sinema Araştırmaları Dergisi*, 2 (2) Güz, pp. 7-31.

Özek, Ali, Hekimoğlu İsmail ve Mesut Uçakan. (2003) "Sanata Genel Bakış ve İslam'da Sanat." *Görsel Sanatlar ve İslam*, İstanbul: ISAV Kitaplığı.

Özgüç, Agah. (2005) *Türlerle Türk Sineması*, İstanbul: Dünya Yayınları.

Özgüç, Agâh. (1993) *100 Filmde Başlangıcından Günümüze Türk Sineması*, Ankara: Bilgi Yayınevi.

Özön, Nijat. (1995) *Karagözden Sinemaya:Türk Sineması ve Sorunları*, cilt 1, Ankara: Kitle Yayınları.

Özön, Nijat. (1983) "Türk Sineması," *Cumhuriyet Dönemi Türkiye Ansiklopedisi*, cilt 7, İstanbul: İletişim Yayınları.

Özön, Nijat. (1985) *Sinema, Uygulayımı, Sanatı, Tarihi*, İstanbul: Hil Yayınları.

Öztürk, Serdar. (2006) "Karagöz Co-Opted: Turkish Shadow Theatre of the Early Republic (1923-1945)," *Asian Theatre Journal*, 23 (2), pp. 292-313.

Öztürk, Serdar. (2005) *Erken Cumhuriyet Döneminde Sinema Seyir Siyaset*, İstanbul: Elips Yayınları.

Özuyar, Ali. (2011) *Faşizmin Etkisinde Türkiye'de Sinema (1939-1945)*, Istanbul: Doruk Yayımcılık.

Özuyar, Ali. (2004) *Babiâli'de Sinema*, Istanbul: İzdüşüm Yayınları.

Pandian, Anand. (2011) "Reel time: Ethnography and the Historical Ontology of the Cinematic Image," *Screen*, 52 (2), pp. 193-214.

Petek, Gaye. (1968) "Devrim ve Sinema," *Genç Sinema*, 1, pp. 5-22.

Perry, John R. (1985) "Language Reform in Turkey and Iran," *International Journal of Middle East Studies*, 17 (3), pp. 295-311.

Poague, Leland. (1985) "Interpretive Models and Ethical Choices: The Example of Film Studies," *Journal of Aesthetic Education*, 19 (4), pp. 21-36.

Polan, Dana B. (1982) "Above All Else to Make You See": Cinema and the Ideology of Spectacle," *Boundary 2*, 11 (1/2), pp. 129-144.

Polan, Dana B. (1981) "Roland Barthes and the Moving Image," *October*, 18, pp. 41-46.

Prendergast, Christopher. (1986) "Cinema Sociology: Cultivating the Sociological Imagination through Popular Film," *Teaching Sociology*, 14 (4), pp. 243-248.

Preis, Eran. (1990) "Not Such A Happy Ending: The Ideology of The Open Ending," *Journal of Film and Video*, 42 (3), pp. 18-23.

Prince, Stephen. (1990) "Power And Pain: Content Analysis And The Ideology Of Pornography," *Journal of Film and Video*, 42 (2), pp. 31-41.

Prince, Stephen. (1996) "True Lies: Perceptual Realism, Digital Images, and Film Theory," *Film Quarterly*, 49 (3), pp. 27-37.

Prince, Stephen. (1988) "The Pornographic Image and the Practice of Film Theory," *Cinema Journal*, 27 (2), pp. 27-39.

Reati, Fernando. (1989) "Argentine Political Violence and Artistic Representation in Films of the 1980's," *Latin American Literary Review*, 17 (34), pp. 24-39.

Refiğ, Halit. (1971) *Ulusal Sinema Kavgası*, Istanbul: Dergah Yayınları.

Resina, Joan Ramon. (1998) "Historical Discourse and the Propaganda Film: Reporting the Revolution in Barcelona," *New Literary History*, 29 (1), pp. 67-84.

Reynolds, Larry J. (1997) "American Cultural Iconography: Vision, History, and the Real," *American Literary History*, 9 (3), pp. 381-395.

Robbe-Grillet, Alain and Bruce Morrissette. (1977) "Critical Order and Disorder in Film and Fiction," *Critical Inquiry*, 4 (1), pp. 1-20.

Roberts, Martin. (1988) "Baraka": World Cinema and the Global Culture Industry," *Cinema Journal*, 37 (3), pp. 62-82.

Robertson, Pamela. (2006) "The Sound of Film Acting," *Journal of Film and Video*, 58 (1/2), pp. 71-83.

Rosen, Philip. (1981) "The Politics of the Sign and Film Theory," *October*, 17, pp. 5-21.

Rosenbaum, Jonathan. (1997) *Movies as Politics*, California&London: University of California Press.

Rothman, William. (2004) *The "I" of The Camera*, 2nd. ed., N.York: Cambridge University Press.

Ruppert, Peter. (1989) "Fassbinder, Spectatorship, and Utopian Desire," *Cinema Journal*, 28 (2), pp. 28-47.

Rustow, Dankwart A. (1973) "The Modernization of Turkey in Historical and Comparative Perspective," ed. K. Karpat, *Social Change and Politics in Turkey: A Structural-Historical Analysis,* Leiden: E. J. Brill Pub.

Rutsky, R. L. and Justin Wyatt. (1990) "Serious Pleasures: Cinematic Pleasure and the Notion of Fun," *Cinema Journal*, 30 (1), pp. 3-19.

Safarian, Alexander. (2004) "Ziya Gökalp on National Education," *Iran & the Caucasus*, 8 (2), pp. 219-229.

Saktanber, Ayşe. (2006) "Women and the Iconography of Fear: Islamization in Post-Islamist Turkey," *Signs*, 32 (1), pp. 21-31.

Sam, Rıza. (2004) "Kitle İletişiminin Tüketim İdeolojisi ya da Üretilen Tiryakiliğin Büyüsü," *Doğu-Batı*, 30, pp. 143-157.

Saxton, Christine. (1986) "The Collective Voice as Cultural Voice," *Cinema Journal*, 26 (1), pp. 19-30.

Saygıner, Hakkı. (1959) "Basın Toplantısı," *Dünya Gazetesi*, 29 Ağustos 1959.

Scheunemann, Dietrich (ed). (2005) *Avant-garde / Neo-avant-garde*, Amsterdam &New York: Rodopi.

Schleiner, Louise. (1999) "Voice, Ideology, and Gendered Subjects: The Case of As You Like It and Two Gentlemen," *Shakespeare Quarterly*, 50 (3), pp. 285-309.

Schneider, Ben Ross Jr. and Edward Pechter. (1988) "The New Historicism," *PMLA*, 103 (1), pp. 60-62.

Scognamillo, Giovanni. (2003) *Türk Sinema Tarihi*, İstanbul: Kabalcı Yayınevi.

Sencer, Yakut. (1979) *Türkiye'de Kentleşme*, 1.Basım, Ankara: Kültür Bakanlığı Yayınları.

Sevinçli, Efdal. (1987) *Meşrutiyet'ten Cumhuriyet'e Sinema'dan Tiyatro'ya Muhsin Ertuğrul*, İstanbul: Broy Yayınları.

Shattuc, Jane. (1993) "Contra" Brecht: R. W. Fassbinder and Pop Culture in the Sixties," *Cinema Journal*, 33 (1), pp. 35-54.

Silberman, Marc. (1987) "The Politics of Representation: Brecht and the Media," *Theatre Journal*, 39 (4), pp. 448-460.

Simpson, Paul. (1993) *Language, Ideology and Point of View*, London & N.York: Routledge.

Smith, Anthony D. (1991) *National Identity*, London: Penguin.

Smith, Murray. (1995) "Film Spectatorship and the Institution of Fiction," *The Journal of Aesthetics and Art Criticism*, 53 (2), pp. 113-127.

Sobchack, Vivian. (2004) *Carnal Thoughts-Embodiment and Moving Image Culture*, L.Angeles & London: University of California Press.

Sobchack, Vivian. (1997) "The Insistent Fringe: Moving Images and Historical Consciousness," *History and Theory*, 36 (4), pp. 4-20.

Sobchack, Vivian C. (1980) "Beyond Visual Aids: American Film as American Culture," *American Quarterly*, 32 (3), pp. 280-300.

Soja, Edward. (1989) *Postmodern Geographies: The Reassertion of Space in Critical Social Theory*, London: Verso.

Soysal, Mümtaz. (1997) *100 Soruda Anayasanın Anlamı*, İstanbul: Gerçek Yayınevi.

Spencer, Robert F. (1958) "Culture Process and Intellectual Current: Durkheim and Atatürk," *American Anthropologist*, 60 (4), pp. 640-657.

Staiger, Janet. (1985) "The Politics of Film Canons," *Cinema Journal*, 24 (3), pp. 4-23.

Stam, Robert, Robert Burgoyne and Sandy Flitterman-Lewis. (1992) *New Vocabularies In Film Semiotics*, London&N.York: Routledge.

Stoddart, Mark C. J. (2007) "Ideology, Hegemony, Discourse: A Critical Review of Theories of Knowledge and Power," *Social Thought and Research*, 28, pp. 191-225.

Stoneman, Rod. (1979) "Film-related Practice And the Avant-garde," *Screen*, 20 (3-4), pp. 40-57.

Suner, Asuman. (2004) "Masum ve Mahsun: 1990'lar Korku Sineması," ed. Deniz Bayraktar, *Türk Film Araştırmalarında Yeni Yönelimler: 4*, 1.Basım, İstanbul: Bağlam Yayınları.

Szyliowicz, Joseph S. (1966) "Political Participation and Modernization in Turkey," *The Western Political Quarterly*, 19 (2), pp. 266-284.

Szyliowicz, Joseph S. (1970) "Students and Politics in Turkey," *Middle Eastern Studies*, 6 (2), pp. 150-162.

Şafak, Elif. (2006) "Accelerating the Flow of Time: Soft Power and the Role of Intellectuals in Turkey," *World Literature Today*, 80 (1), pp. 24-26.

Şasa, Ayşe. (1993) *Yeşilçam Günlüğü*, İstanbul: Dergâh Yayınları.

Şasa, Ayşe. (2003) *Yeşilçam Günlüğü*, İstanbul: Gelenek Yayınları.

Şen, Abdurrahman (ed). (2010) *Türk Sinemasında Yerli Arayışlar*, Ankara: Kültür ve Turizm Bakanlığı.

Şentürk, Ridvan. (2011) *Postmodern Kaos ve Sinema*, Istanbul: Avrupa Yakası Yayıncılık.

Tachau Frank and Metin Heper. (1983) "The State, Politics, and the Military in Turkey," *Comparative Politics*, 16 (1), pp. 17-33.

Taylor, Norman. (1996) "Re-presenting the Field of Restricted Cultural Production: the Nude at the Interface," *Screen*, 37 (1), pp. 16-29.

Teshome, H.Gabriel. (1986) "Colonialism and 'Law and Order' Criticism," *Screen*, 27 (3-4), pp. 140-148.

Tosun, Necip. (1992) *Mesut Uçakan'la Sinema Söyleşileri*, İstanbul: Nehir Yayınları.

Tunç, Nazif. (2010) "Sinemamızda Yerli Yönelişler Neden Gerekir?" ed. Abdurrahman Şen, *Türk Sinemasında Yerli Arayışlar*, Ankara: Kültür ve Turizm Bakanlığı.

Turan, Ömer. (2007) "Takva ya da Oryantalist Kiliselerin Ötesi ... ," Birikim, 213, pp. 90-93.

Türk, İbrahim. (2001) *Halit Refiğ-Düşlerden Düşüncelere Söyleşiler*, İstanbul: Kabalcı Yayınevi.

Uçakan, Mesut. (2007) *Türk Sinemasında İdeoloji*, İstanbul: Düşünce Yayınları.

Uçakan, Mesut. (2010) *Türk Sinemasında İdeoloji*, İstanbul: Sepya Yayıncılık.

Ufuk, Adnan ve Mümtaz Osman. (1995) "Türkiye'de Devrimci Sinema Tartışmaları 1," *Görüntü*, Türk Sineması Özel Sayısı, 4, pp. 6-17.

Uyar, Mehmet. (2010) "Öncü Yönetmen:Yücel Çakmaklı," ed. Abdurrahman Şen, *Türk Sinemasında Yerli Arayışlar*, Ankara: Kültür ve Turizm Bakanlığı.

Ülman, A. Haluk and Frank Tachau. (1965) "Turkish Politics: The Attempt to Reconcile Rapid Modernization with Democracy," *Middle East Journal*, 19 (2), pp. 153-168.

Van Dijk, T.A. (1998) *Ideology: A Multidisciplinary Approach*, London: Sage Publication.

Volosinov, V.N. (1996) "Marxism and the Philosophy of Language," eds. Charles Harrison and Paul Wood, *Art in Theory, 1900–1990: An Anthology of Changing Ideas*, Oxford: Blackwell.

Waldman, Diane. (1977) "Critical Theory and Film: Adorno and "The Culture Industry," *New German Critique*, 12, pp. 39-60.

Walsh, Michael. (1996) "National Cinema, National Imaginary," *Film History*, 8 (1), pp. 5-17.

Watts, Philip. (2005) "Roland Barthes's Cold-War Cinema," *SubStance*, 34 (3), pp. 17-32.

Wayne, Mike (ed). (2005) *Understanding Film: Marxist Perspectives*, London: Pluto Press.

Williams, Christopher. (1971) "Politics and Production," *Screen*, 12 (4), pp. 6-24.

Williams, Raymond. (1983) *Keywords: A Vocabulary of Culture and Society*, New York: Oxford University Press.

Willemen, Paul. (1972) "On Realism in the Cinema," *Screen*, 13 (1), pp. 37-44.

Wood, Robin. (1976) *Personal Views: Explorations in Film*, London: Gordon Fraser Pub.

Worland, Rick. (1995) "Politics, Film Studies, and The Academy: A Commentary," *Journal of Film and Video*, 46 (4), pp. 42-56.

Yalsızuçanlar, Sadık. (2010) "Türk Sinemasında Yerli Bir Damar: Yücel Çakmaklı," ed. Abdurrahman Şen, *Türk Sinemasında Yerli Arayışlar*, Ankara: Kültür ve Turizm Bakanlığı.

Yavuz, M.Hakan. (2009) *Secularism and Muslim Democracy in Turkey*, N.York: Cambridge University Press.

Yaylagül, Levent. (2004) "1960–1970 Dönemi Türk Sinemasında Düşünce Akımları," ed. Fatma Dalay Küçükkurt ve Ahmet Gürata, *Sinemada Anlatı ve Türler*, Ankara: Vadi Yayınları.

Yeğen, Mesut. (1999) *Devlet Söyleminde Kürt Sorunu*, İstanbul: İletişim Yayınları.

Yenen, İbrahim. (2012) "Türk Sineması'nda İslam(cılık) Pratiği: Milli Sinema Örneği," *İnsan ve Toplum Bilimleri Araştırmaları Dergisi*, III, pp. 240-271.

Yıldırım, Tunç. (2010) "1950'ler Sinema Ortamında Şakir Sırmalı'nın Söyleminin Etkisi," *Sine Cine: Sinema Araştırmaları Dergisi*, Bahar 1, pp. 5-44.

Zhang, Yingjin. (2004) *Chinese National Cinema*, N.York&London: Routledge.

Zimmer, Christian and Lee Leggett. (1974) "All Films Are Political," *SubStance*, 3 (9), pp. 123-136.

Zizek, Slavoj. (1989) *The Sublime Object of Ideology*, London&N.York: Verso Pub.